INTO THE DEEP

A Writer's Look at Creativity

SUSAN McBRIDE ELS

D1363724

HEINEMANN

PORTSMOUTH, NEW HAMPSHIRE

Heinemann
A division of Reed Elsevier Inc.
361 Hanover Street
Portsmouth, NH   03801-3912

Offices and agents throughout the world

Library of Congress Cataloging-in-Publication Data

Els, Susan McBride.
    Into the deep: a writer's look at creativity / Susan McBride Els.
      p.   cm.
    Includes bibliographical references.
    ISBN 0-435-08803-3 (alk. paper)
    1. Authorship. 2. Creation (Literary, artistic, etc.) I. Title.
PN145.E62   1994
808'.02—dc20
                                  93-44802
                                     CIP

Acquistions Editor: Toby Gordon
Production Editor: Vicki Kasabian
Text and cover design: Joyce Weston
Cover photograph: Joyce Weston

Printed in the United States of America on acid-free paper
98 97 96 95 94   BB   1 2 3 4 5

TO MY FAMILY,

EACH SINGULAR, RARE ONE.

BUT ESPECIALLY MOM,

DAD, AND MY DUDDY DUO.

❦ CONTENTS ❦

❦ ACKNOWLEDGMENTS ❦

I would rather shout my thanks from the top of nearby Camel's Hump mountain. Instead, they are muffled here in pages readers thumb over to find the book's beginning. But, for me, the book began—and now begins—with these names:

David and Japhet, who ate an unpalatable number of Mrs. Fry's frozen chicken pot pies so I could go to graduate school.

Pat Cordeiro, Pat Davidson, and Nina Greenwald of the Critical and Creative Thinking program at the University of Massachusetts, who delicately pressed a would-be storyteller into the scholar's mold just long enough to finish a thesis. And Delores Gallo, whose class coaxed the words "I am a writer."

Toby Gordon, publishing director at Heinemann, who let my manuscript sit on her desk until it spoke to her and then listened to me as well.

Alan Huisman, my Heinemann editor, who generously poured his scant time and thoughtful precision into the manuscript.

Bill Oakes, an inspired painter, friend, and teacher, who shares a zeal for sea-smoothed granite stones and creative connections. Special thanks for his all-important connection to Toby Gordon at Heinemann.

Mom and Dad, a rare blend of proof-reader and pleasure-reader both of this book and their daughter.

And my sister, Bunny—the real writer—who, at all hours, is willing to read and listen to unformed writing-in-process. She has taught and encouraged me far beyond the boundaries of this book.

❦ INTRODUCTION ❦

❦ ❦ ❦

THE CALL OF THE JUNGLE

I write. It's that simple.

However, against this straight and sturdy fence pushes a jungle of complication and contradiction. Sometimes I look over the fence. The unruly ways and means behind the writing call me to explore. But I answer that I don't want to look into why and how I write. I don't want to be snarled in process. I just want to write.

Possibly it's the same with you. Perhaps your own jungle intrudes on your work. You hold your back to it and hack off its occasional creeping vines and continue writing. You keep the fence line clear and your land productive. Scouting the wilds behind your writing would surely be diverting and probably be purposeless.

Maybe you fear the jungle. Maybe you believe that tangling in the mysteries of why and how you work will kill the work. You're not alone.

Perhaps a safer alternative is to climb over someone

else's fence. However reluctant we might be to explore our own processes, we can trek down the paths of other writers and keep our psyches comfortably removed. We can take from their explorations what will help us and refuse whatever will disrupt our work. If nothing else, we will gain the comfort of company through unmarked land.

This book is a personal response to calls from the thickets bordering my own writing work—calls to explore creativity as well as writing. What follows may therefore also be of interest to artists other than writers.

So put away the ax. Clip the barbed-wire defenses. You have nothing to lose. This isn't your jungle.

PART ONE

Elements of Creativity

❦ ONE ❦

Water

Many fiction writers keep untidy journals to scratch in at day's end or fumble for at inspired moments. These journals are multipurposed: they seal the seeds of intuition and image that will germinate in the soil of later work; they record insights about the writing craft; they vent frustration and work out meaning; and when nothing else inspires work, they can jump-start the weak-willed into productive writing spells.

When I began to write a novel, I started a new kind of diary on the side. Unlike my previous journals, this one was to focus on the creative process that would mother—or, perhaps, beat—a story into the world. As a master's degree candidate, my plan was to match the writing process recorded in my journal to the ideas of contemporary creativity theorists.

My first entry in the gray, linen-bound process notebook spoke resolutely of "this experiment in creativity, where I can watch the creative process at work and follow some of the hidden tunnels—the intricacies of ideas and modes of thought—that lead to the finished product."

But that was to be the *sole* entry in my official journal. Because of the messy nature of creativity, the "journal" immediately degenerated into ubiquitous scraps of paper stuck between the seats of my car, magnetized to the stove exhaust hood, "filed" in drawers. Two sizes of pink and green Post-It Notes turned my office walls and windows into a sloppy mosaic. There was nothing organized about this process diary. Sure, the methodic notes taken while I worked at the computer marched in formation onto labeled disks. But the really good stuff, which came while walking, driving, and cooking, was hanging around my life like suspended confetti.

This surface shift from neat journal to confetti notes barely hinted at the yawning rift underground.

When I began writing the novel, I ceased to be a creativity student. I became a storyteller. Prior to taking on this "experiment," I simply did not consider the gap between the two. As a writer who needed a student project, I would use the novel as a showcase of invention and problem solving that involved creative techniques and skills. Armed with knowledge of the creative processes, I would report on the run the how, when, and why of storymaking. I guessed that an account of a novel's creation would probably support existing creativity theory and maybe discover new ground.

Disaster sneaked up with the force of a neap tide. After months of writing both the novel and its process notes, I stood ready to begin my thesis. Blissfully unaware of the impending crisis, I printed the computer notes from disks onto neat, numbered pages. I read them slowly at first, then faster. I began scanning, anxiously flipping through the pages, searching for something I could use in my thesis. Panic. I had done it wrong!

What I read seemed foreign. It did not match what I felt my writing experience to be. Although a few peak experiences dotted the landscape, the notes were mostly boring, run-on reports of floundering and regaining footing, wondering where the story was going, following trails of connections and associations among ideas, and talking to myself about who the characters were.

As a student of creativity, I was ashamed. Most of what I had learned about creativity was missing. There were no appropriate accounts of the creative personality and its independence, its drive for excellence, its willingness to take risks, its intrinsic motivation. The notes neglected to refer to problem-solving strategies, problem redefinition, methods for keeping response options open, working at the edge. How could my process record be so inappropriate to the focus of my thesis?

There was nothing to do but incite the student in me to grab the storyteller by the lapels and wrest some psychological sense from these notes. It must be in there somewhere.

It was. I poured my notes and recollections through the sieve of creativity theories. But in straining out process stages, creative skills, heuristics, and personality traits, I felt the shadowy essence of my work slip away. This saddened me. I yearned for that essence.

My confetti notes, however, taken at odd moments—moments I had never considered legitimate writing time—were different. They captured flash insights and deep ponderings. They expressed what I felt about writing as it entwined around life. They seemed genuine and familiar. And I sensed that somewhere within them lay that shadowy essence of my process. I became obsessed with this undefined heart that I believed my notes were trying to reveal.

In a renewed search, I expanded my subject to include not only the novel but *anything* I was writing—essays, poetry, short fiction, this book, even the process notes themselves. To maintain sanity while I schizophrenically wrote and watched myself watch the process, I stopped trying to analyze "how," and simply jotted down random thoughts that occurred while I was writing. And I wrote more notes on the side in odd moments. The result was a record of experience more than process.

But sorting all these confetti notes was like working a diabolical puzzle: there were no corners or sides with distinctive straight edges to tip me off. To fit these into a cohesive, complete presentation was an impossible dream. I faced a 10,000-piece puzzle with only a short summer and a card table. What I needed was eternal life and the floor of the Astrodome.

However, from the fatty flesh of notes and unformed recollections clear themes eventually worked their way out like slivers from the palm of the hand. These themes concerned the dark, watery nature of elemental creativity—vague images, premonitions, powerful potentials, intuition, insight, inspiration and motivation, time and self falling away, a sense of sacredness, how the artist stands in relation to the work. These were not the rock-solid, squared-off, easy-to-build-with components I was accustomed to as a creativity student. When I tried to grasp them, they slipped through my mental fingers. They would not hold their shape, but tended to flow into one another. I was up to my neck in water with no dry land in sight.

The deep. Artists avoid talking about it. Open the back of a camera, and the film is exposed to bright sunlight. It loses its sensitivity forever. It is ruined. In order to work its magic, film is meant to be shut tight in the black box. So, many artists believe, should the deep creative processes be kept in the shadows, revered but never probed, believed but never comprehended.

Unlike these artists, many creativity theorists steeped in cognitive psychology—along with contemporary Western culture in general—simply deny the deep. Creativity has come to mean problem solving and innovation based on rational techniques and skills.

But Eastern cultures perceive creativity as springing from a deeper source than rational thinking. From an Eastern view, thinking is only an extension of the limited senses that play on the hard surfaces of life. Other ways of knowing enable the mind to dip beneath the surface sources of originality and ladle out the nectar of creation. These other ways of knowing are often grouped loosely under intuition.

In its pursuit of "how-to" creativity that can be packaged and sold in textbooks and seminars, Western-style theory says of intuition and its mystery, "Oh, that's just how it *feels*. It's not how it *works*." "How it works" means rational processes such as planning, selecting, judging, manipulating techniques and schemata—the stuff gleaned from "talk-aloud" reports given by artists in the process of creating in the laboratory. "How it works" exiles intuition and its culture of inspiration, insight, listening, faith, empathy, serendipity, and other deepwater currents that direct the creative process.

As I pored over my confetti notes and remembered experiences of writing, "how it feels" emerged as primary. This felt experience motivated my work and defined my process. Knowing more about "how it feels"—swimming in the deep, dark waters—helped my work. Analyzing the mundane "how it works" processes according to cognitive psychology was irrelevant.

Founded on the old model of the brain as information-processing computer, cognitive psychological research into the nuts and bolts of creative thinking is helpful in teaching problem-solving and idea-generating techniques. Certainly, creative work, like any work, depends upon finely tuned rational thinking and technical skills. But without a heavy dose of the felt experience of creation, psychology will never promote true creativity.

New thinking in physics is actually more promotive of imagination and originality, because it embraces "unscience"—those traditionally nonscientific notions of mystery, transcendence, the acceptance of paradox, serendipity, the overlap between objective reality and the truth in myth and dreams.

Perhaps the difference between creativity researchers and artists lies in the disparity of the realities they are trying to get at. Theorists chase fireflies into the daylight in order to study them under microscopes and dissect them with the scalpel of rational empiricism; practicing artists want and need to know fireflies whole, in the dark. The intellect's blazing rationalism must be darkened somewhat for the heart to see the true essences. I am not saying the biologist's painstaking study of the firefly under the light of science is unappreciated or not useful to the artist—on the contrary. However, during creative work, that knowledge must serve in the shadow of intuition. In the twilight of the deep the artist—informed by inspiration, faith, hope, intuition—can see the clear reflection of forms that would disappear under pure, limited rationalism. "How it feels" is and must be primary to the artist. If we attend to "how it works," our writing, dancing, painting—all the works of the soul—will shrivel.

❦ T W O ❦

Wind

W ind Breath Spirit
These three fuse into one in the old tongues: in
Hebrew, *ruwach*; in Greek, *pneuma*; in Latin, *spiritus*.

The wind riffles the water's surface; a spirit blows
over the creative deep. This spirit breathes potential. It
inspires with its promise of something lurking where just
a moment ago there was nothing. We do not know the
origin of this stirring spirit and we cannot articulate its
language. But we feel its presence. Like infants searching
for breast milk, we suck at the air for its elusive potential.
And with the drawing of each breath, the potential gathers form.

But the experience of inspiration is not so much that
we are breathing; it is more that we are being breathed.

✥ ✥ ✥

INSPIRATION

Falling in Love

Have you ever watched a rescuer give mouth-to-mouth resuscitation? He blows breath into the victim, whose lungs rise and fall with the rescuer's own air. I have never been rescued (in this manner), but I have heard of the exhilaration one feels at the breath of renewed life. When a foreign breath blows through us, we quicken. Life tastes fresh. Light intensifies our vision. For a time. But soon the inspiration becomes our own breath. Its newness stales. Its energy recedes. We wait for the next inspiration.

I know that inspiration is not conjured up. It comes as a gift from someone, somewhere, something outside us. We can court it, receive it, attend to it, but rational thought cannot command, infer, debate, or judge it. This intuitive nature of inspiration sets the character for the creative process. The ideas that forward creation, that bring form to potential, *visit* the artist. She does not make them; she entertains them in a hospitable context, before reason comes to bear.

Inspiration is the sudden, noticeable movement of something that has been lying still. It is the first nudge toward a creative act that draws light and meaning out of the infinite pool of mystery and darkness. It is not an idea but rather is a force moving the artist's mind toward creative discovery and expression.

Inspiration slakes our continual thirst for newness upon newness. Yet nothing is really new; rather, it is a new expression, outgrowth, or rendition of the old. Newness always leaves an aftertaste of something ancient. What seems and feels new is *original*—a fresh bubbling from primal, unorganized elements, from the deep, the source of newness.

We must ascend into a certain sacred wildness—the place beyond man's tidy, controlled, and largely false world. And this wildness, although it threatens our habitual, sturdy thought structures, is the source of new structures, new patterns, new beauty and meaning. It has more in common with prayer than with mind-altering psychologies or substances. It's an awakening, a pure oxygen sweeping out our littered consciousness, a heightened awareness that sees beyond the seeing. It has often been characterized as love. Falling in love sharpens our perceptions: the outlines of the winter trees are crisper, the summer air caresses more softly, the sky's blue vibrates, and everyone seems kinder and better. Inspiration is falling in love, falling out of the limited, crowded, everyday mind into a larger perception.

The Powerful Vagueness and the Pleasurable Nag

As soon as we stepped off the street onto the uneven wood floors, I felt it. The smells of two centuries permeated the posts and hung from the beams. Inside the dim barn a crowd of summer people lingered around the carousel, waving at family and strangers who drifted by on wooden horses. Somewhere in the slow, rhythmical circling of the carousel's "flying horses," time skipped its track and slipped sideways. The bright, thumping music dulled. I was alone, suspended, while everything about me kept moving. I remember standing utterly still, thinking that if a muscle twitched, this fragile moment of eternity would jerk back on track and something important would vanish before I could grab hold of it. I didn't care that I looked the innocent fool. (Process notes)

That moment incited a novel. In that barn, I experienced more than a roused sentiment. I was convinced some outside force was pulling on me, yanking me toward feelings, images, and meaning that only a story could explore and illuminate. This utter conviction characterizes inspiration.

But the conviction came shrouded.

When we say, "It was an inspiration!" we often mean that an idea struck with such sudden and complete definition that it only had to be copied in the flesh, *et voilà!* However, the carousel inspiration was typical for me in its powerful *vagueness*. Inspiration is intuitive rather than rational. Even though my perception of my intuitions is uncertain, they inspire me with consummate conviction. They exude wholeness and richness but lack detail. They make me edgy with the uneasiness that I am forgetting something. I trust the misplaced object or forgotten idea *is*; I just don't know *where* or *what* it is. But I will recognize it when I see it. This "forgotten" feeling is the power base of potential. It's a pleasant but nagging impulse to discovery.

The obscurity of such intuitions used to bother me. I would spend time trying to define them, clarify them, find their edges and center before engaging the writing. I ached for a clear, fully drawn inspiration in order to begin writing. I didn't realize that the *vagueness* and *strong potential* of inspiration activate a force—mysterious and magnetic—that pulls the work forward. I must write my way toward the fulfillment of the inspiration's potential. There is no shortcut.

Not analysis of intuitions but their creative expression is the path to clarifying the potential. When we circumvent the creative work—the painting, writing, composing, dreaming, playing, dancing—by probing and analyzing the inspiration directly, we are philosophers, psychologists, scientists, thinkers—but not artists. If the rational mind has its way before intuitive expression begins, the inspiration will wither and no creative expression will result. Creative work comes in the back door, never confronting the inspiration head-on, but coaxing it indirectly through intuition.

Long-Winded Inspirations versus "Puffs"

Some inspirations require time and breathing room before their potential grows strong enough to induce creative work; others need to be snatched immediately.

Today I wrote a poem in a way that seemed unusual to me. It came too easily. I had just finished filling the bird feeder. Something about pouring in the seed and watching for the birds afterward struck me. I knew it was a poem. It was such a sweet, simple inspiration that I trusted it to the writing process immediately. I spent no time considering or analyzing it, but went straight to the desk to find it in the writing. I glanced out the window as I wrote, trying to hold onto the fleeting thing that had inspired me. In about an hour I had found the poem:

FEBRUARY ABSOLUTION

For three weeks
I neglected the bird feeder.

But now, hanging heavy with seed
it bobs in green-feathered pine
like a buoy in evening waters
waiting.

I feel its rhythm
bowing within me
making supplication
to the uninhabited air.

In joyful swoop and staccato peck
Reckless white flashes
spread, like glittering sun across the sea

and chickadees throng my bird feeder
in unrestrained forgiveness.   (Process notes)

This experience taught me something about responding to inspiration. Often, inspirations that impress me as potential poems are complicated and multifaceted gems that grow like crystals in time-lapse films. The original impulse gathers speed and spins out of control before I can begin to write. And because the accretion of ideas is too bulky, too complex, to fit into a poem, the writing grows laborious and frustrating and unfulfilled.

But this time, I did not allow time for the complications to amass. I began writing immediately. The work of the poem rode on the energy of the vaguely glimpsed potential and defined it in a way that, for me, matched the promise of the energizing inspiration.

However, although the powerful vagueness often strikes whole, prompting an immediate effort at creative expression, inspiration just as often needs time to ripen before it can initiate creative work. It may gather completeness only through successive pulses.

My mind's working on a book of essays about wildflowers . . . just vague feelings about science and mysticism now . . .   (Process notes, July 1990)

I think the stuff I'm trying to say in the wildflower book is really about fields in general. There's a compelling feeling about "the field."   (September 1990)

Well, it's getting clearer. It's the *night* fields I want to write about ... (December 1990)

A day or so after that last journal entry, I was browsing through the nature section in a bookstore when I was hit—out of the blue, not from a bookshelf—with the words "Midnight Naturalist." They came without warning. This final stage of inspiration held enough promise to propel the idea for an adventure-after-dark story about Max and the Midnight Naturalist. It was a complete (but of course undefined) vision of a tale based on a spunky old man. The tone of the character and the story was strong though still inarticulate. But I was convinced that the story or stories (for I had already begun to see this as a series) stood whole, waiting for me to discover them. If I had launched into writing before I felt a conviction and a sense of completeness, I might have floundered around for days and finally given up, judging the inspiration a dud.

So, I learned from the quick poem and the delayed series of stories that the writing must begin at the point of whole inspiration. I need only develop a sensitivity to this point, to detect the right moment to dive into the creative work. This sense of completeness—whether it pounces suddenly or evolves subtly—is what instigates the creative work. Ripening occurs naturally when I attend to the inspiration rather than analyze it. If I give it a wide place in the shadows of my mind, I believe it will find its form and emerge when the time is right.

Inspiration Can Backfire

During my early years of writing, if a full-blown inspiration knocked me over with its clarity and definition, I fell for it. But I've learned that when the fuel ignites prematurely, the engine will probably backfire.

> Had another long talk with Alec across the street today. It always surprises me how tall and straight he is when I get up close to him. It's not hard to imagine him a strapping young Navy officer. But his eyes are nearly gone now, and he talks only of memories. Today he spoke again of children. Always the children. What a wonderful father he would have been! His thoughts were on two barefooted rascals he met in port on a day off from the war. He took pictures of each on the promise of a dime after the boys received the prints. For months no dimes came in the mail. Alec's ship buddies laughed it off saying, "Who'd expect two poor kids to pay up?" Alec did. Out of love. And faith in kids. Two months later the dimes came— along with the explanation that the boys had needed to save enough returnable bottles to get the coins. They were sorry it had taken so long. Alec beamed at me. "I wonder what those boys are doin' now!"
>
> (Process notes)

This backyard exchange inspired me with complete and clear energy. It was not vague. I knew exactly what to do with it. That night, I jotted down bits of Alec's mini-adventures with kids for a trio of essays to be titled "Alec's War Stories."

But I never wrote the essays. The inspiration was too highly delineated. The stories were finished in my mind before they reached paper. The sense of potential necessary to sustain the desire to write them had dissipated. The travels I had taken in my imagination were overdeveloped and fully explored. I canceled the trip.

Intuition versus Emotion

If we can't distinguish intuition from emotion, inspiration will cheat us.

Like intuition, emotion is a movement of the mind. But what I will call "emotion" is energy excited much as the body is excited by sensation. It's usually a response—anger, joy, sorrow, sympathy—to familiar, maybe habitual, stimuli. I use the term "intuition" to apply to *new* impulses that move the mind to fresh feeling and understanding.

Sometimes I can sense the difference simply because emotion often leads to wallowing rather than writing. I just want to hang surrounded by the feeling. I imagine it is a poem. But I don't write it. Emotion can be hackneyed, predictable. Inspiration feels neither predictable nor repetitive; it feels fresh, unused. And because of this utter newness, I am *moved* into expression.

However, *high* emotion can generate creative expression as forcefully as intuition. The good thing about strong emotion is that it needs relief. I can't wallow for more than a few days before yearning overtakes the pleasure, sorrow permeates the joy, and something must be done. I can either throw myself into another life or write.

But the writing that springs from emotion is different from the writing propelled by intuition.

> I've been cheated by Pavarotti—what a schlep I've had, thanks to his singing "Nessun Dorma." Yeah, I guess you could say I got into it. I was so overwhelmed with the music and the Italian (what's great about Italian is you don't have to know it to understand it), that I felt I just *had* to write about it. It took pages of schmaltzy, gagging, sentimental mush to tell me this was no inspiration. I was a dupe to pure emotion. But, I did end up writing a *comical* essay—in total befuddlement, because what I was writing had no genetic relation to the tragic, yearning emotion I was feeling from "Nessun Dorma." (Process notes)

Here is the cheat: emotional inspiration may not lead the artist to itself but to something wholly incongruous, unrelated. It tricks us into mistaking an energy source for a writing topic.

Emotions inspire not by their potential, but by their passion. An intuitive inspiration calls the artist with a promise of something to be discovered—of meaning, feelings, wisdom that can be gained only through creative expression—in my case, through a story, poem, or essay.

We write *toward* intuitive inspiration's potential. We write *from* emotional inspiration. Emotion is a centrifugal force pushing us to creativity for relief's sake; intuition is a centripetal force pulling us toward a potential for discovery's sake.

The Divine Bigness

Often I mistake the momentum of a potential or the reach of an emotion. I am sure its promise or passion will lead to exalted and stirring writing. There's a story of a Chinese emperor who had the same problem with a piece of rare jade. He asked his sculptor to carve a mountain and a waterfall from the stone. The sculptor returned with a depiction of a little fish and some pebbles. The emperor was angry. "What did you do with my jade?" The sculptor answered, "Your Majesty, there was no mountain or waterfall in that jade. There was only a fish and some pebbles" (Moyers).

Always in my mind the inspiration speaks a mountain and a waterfall. And always I'm left with a tiny fish and a few pebbles. For a long time I was disappointed and frustrated.

It's both humbling and freeing to learn that the rare, highly valued inspirations often generate disappointing creations. Is it lack of genius that causes a creation to fall short? Or is it overblown expectations that are to blame? We must grow into readiness before our best inspirations can lead us to rare and valued expression. And it is well to remember Blake, who saw "a World in a Grain of Sand"

and "a Heaven in a Wild Flower"; he recommends we look for the divine bigness in everyday minutiae.

It's important to consider our readiness often. But we will do that naturally in the practice of our art. Much as the painter's eye perceives a range of values within one color, we will come to sense the relative demands of inspiration. Sometimes the shadow of an insight moves across my mind. I know it is big. But it portends a work I am not prepared to execute. I must wait. Writers with far more sensitivity and power of expression have wept on hearing calls they could not answer.

Many inspirations are never to be written about or written from; they are neither a topic nor an energy source for creative response. Like many writers, probably, I am eager to recognize any strong feeling as a holy summons to write. But there are times to separate writing implements from inspiration.

Where did *this* come from? I'm driving to the grocery store, kind of forgetting where I'm going, and I'm struck with this sudden feeling of the wholeness of things. I have to pull off the road. Everything seems "of a piece" as Nanny used to say about landscape painting. But I'm not just seeing the landscape that way. It's the whole *world* that feels right. All its thoughts, its yearnings, its love, its purposes, and desires. All connected and safe. I feel sure it's true. It's very clear and yet, at the same time, vague and general. I don't know what it means. But I want to. I feel content. Now I understand why some people say, "I could die now and it would be alright." That's good. And that's bad. But the feeling's good. (Process notes)

This was provocative contemplation, not a writing propellant. Its purpose was to feed the lake from which future intuitions and emotions would spring to produce creative work.

The pleasurable nag assumes a different style. Productive inspirations often irritate more than they inspire. They *bully* us into a creative workout.

Why can't I leave the story about the dwergs alone! I hate it. I'm tired of it. It's been hanging around like that galling, impudent guy with the 1965 MG who kept promising I could drive, so I kept going out with him—even though I never got more than a couple of blocks down Mass Ave. (So I hit every drain grate. Big deal.) A familiar promise keeps knocking at the door telling me there's a great story here. What is compelling me? Why do I keep going out on these rides to nowhere? This muse is just making himself a habit. He has no intention of taking me to the real story anymore than that guy was going to let me drive to the end of Mass Ave. I've gotta bury this one. Maybe.

(Process notes)

Even pleasant intuitions are two-faced generals. They enlist and inspire us just so we will follow them into battle. At some point, inspiration is joined by torment.

❦ ❦ ❦

TROUBLING

If an intuition is more than a passing emotion, it begins to push me. It presses toward expression, form. Initially, I feel energized and confident. During errands and while cooking dinner, at school meetings and the grocery store, I am preparing for writing. I feel the potential grow to embrace images and metaphors, tones of dialogue, possible events and characters' responses to those events. But the moment I slip in front of the computer to write seriously, I don't want to. I want to walk or call a friend or play the piano. I *know* it is desk time. I *know* the book, essay, or short story will not be written at the post office or in the car.

One morning I sincerely considered my problem of sitting at the desk: how to stave off the small but deadly temptations to get a drink of water, to put a load of clothes in the washer, to vacuum the family room. Embarrassed at my unimaginative solution, I nevertheless tied myself to the chair with an old bathrobe sash. I made complex knots, figuring the time required to untie them would give me a moment to reconsider my temptation. It didn't work. Neighbors, opinion pollsters, friends of the environment, the water-meter reader, rang at the door downstairs. I wearied of tying and untying and couldn't fit through the door with the chair strapped on.

That very night I was stunned by a radio interview with John McPhee. What did he do to discipline himself to sit and write? asked the interviewer. Well, when he was *very young and inexperienced,* he threaded his bathrobe belt through the spindles of his chair and tied himself in. It didn't work for him either.

This is the beginning of the "troubling." It's an apt word. I find little that is comforting or pleasant at this stage of creation. And leaving the desk, or never getting to it in the first place, merely hints at troubling's many dimensions. Most typically, as I scramble up that initial wall of resistance, I'm met by fiends and demons running battle drills in the inner courtyard. Their purpose is to deflate inspiration or to engage in some psychological writer-bashing.

> What made me think I could do this? What's inspired me is way, way beyond my powers of expression. It seemed so simple at its inception. That's the trouble with inspiration—it inspires you not only with the wonder of an idea, but also with an inflated sense of your ability to do something with the idea. I should go looking for some more attainable inspiration.

> What a hoax this idea turned out to be! Filling me with this strong feeling of potential—Ha! The more I look at it, the less impressive it is. It's dwindling before my eyes. I write, but the words just disappear into the paper. Nothing. That's what it was. Nothing.

> (Process notes)

Thus, the sudden, utterly convincing wave of inspiration that lifted me high on its crest of potential now plunges me into the hollow on the other side. The struggle for inspiration and self-confidence continues right to the end. Some writers have only one battle plan: Plow into the writing until a certain momentum kicks in and the writing feeds itself. Don't wait for inspiration; write yourself into it. Sometimes that works for me. Often, though, I write myself into circles and webs until I'm thoroughly tangled with no way out. That only adds confusion to discouragement. It is not always enough simply to write. The most effective weapon I've found is a firm grasp on inspiration, attention, and purpose. And I sharpen this weapon daily by reflecting on and affirming why I write. When we sharpen a knife, we actually realign the atoms along the edge. An artist's continual reconsideration of her place and purpose and personal process realigns—sharpens—her creative edge, thus enabling it to slice through the obstacles, frustration, and resistance separating her from the work.

Thankfully, it's not always like this. Once in a while the writing flows—usually when I'm attempting a simple poem or mini-essay or book review. It happens just often enough to be taken seriously. I float into the illusion that if my writing life is long enough, it will eventually become pure pleasure.

WOW! Now this is a great story idea. It'll be different this time. The birth, for once, is going easily and quickly—this baby will pop right out like a wet grape squeezed between my fingers. This is how it should be: when the inspiration's strong and clear enough, it wings the work toward it, without stress, without agony. Pure joy. Just what writing should be. And, of course, if it's happening now, it can happen again. Right? And again? . . . maybe even become a habit?

(Journal)

Well, not quite:

There's a stench in this holy swamp. A simple thought can easily skew a stable frame of mind into amazing complexity and confusion. I'm thrashing around in a mind filled with extraneous and unrelated thoughts, too many vague ideas of direction, self-doubt, confusion, and general stewing. I want to get out.

When I write, the original inspiration seems to unfurl away from me like a parachute thrown out of the jump plane. It's escaping me even as I grasp for it.

(Process notes)

Here, the troubling becomes distinct from the avoidance and resistance caused by deflated inspiration or collapsed self-confidence. Having gotten past feeling betrayed by inspiration or simply overwhelmed by it, we run smack into the doubting, stewing, groping, tracking and backtracking, the finishing and scrapping of sentences, characters, and ideas. (Do professionals really do this? Is it possible I just need more practice?)

Even when inspiration leads easily and directly to writing, what initially seems solid ground will soon quake with uncertainty. This is the sign of intuition. Intuition is defined as knowledge gained from within rather than from experience—that is, "gut feelings" or instinctive knowing. Intuition in the form of inspiration—the force *energizing* and calling for a creative response—is powerful, full of momentum, convincing, demanding. However, as the force *guiding* the creative work, intuition adjusts its touch. Its energy becomes more persistent than explosive. It speaks softly, requiring our careful attention. It leads indirectly, requiring our patience and an affinity for discovery rather than destination. The inspiring intuition is confident, assured. The guiding intuition is a measure of faith barely surviving doubt and uncertainty.

Of course, inspiration and intuition are inextricably bound together. Beyond a point, it's not useful to divide them. But throughout creative work an energizing inspiration and a guiding intuition work as partners with distinct functions. Guiding intuition assumes a yin-yang identity: the generally good feel of being pulled forward and the generally bad feel of troubling.

Chaos theory, the new kid on the science block, has its own word for troubling: perturbation. At any time, a perfectly stable, simple system can develop a wobble capable of bringing it down. Yet, the possibility of perturbation, the lack of stability, is the paradoxical key to an evolution toward more viable forms of higher order. The perturbation leads to a creative process.

Indeed, Nobel physical chemist Ilya Prigogine perceives chaos as brimming with potential order. And one of his favorite experiments—the Bénard cells—illustrates creative process as well as chemical laws.

When a pan of water is heated from the bottom, the heat is conducted from the lower to the upper surface smoothly and regularly. The water is stable (or "near-equilibrium" in chaos theory terms). As the heat increases, however, the difference in temperature between the bottom and top layers of water also increases. The water reacts turbulently, bubbling and creating eddies that move against the flow. The result is chaos (or "far-from-equilibrium"). Then, at a critical point, the turbulence suddenly shifts into convection currents that form a perfect hexagonal lattice pattern called the Bénard cells.

Chaos offers the potential of order, and the seeming void of the deep offers the potential of creation. When the wind troubles the waters, there is chaos. But this random, uncomfortable turbulence is temporary. It grows toward a sudden shift into patterned waves. Although the waves will at some time again dissipate into turbulence, some law operates within this random troubling.

Chaos theorists refer to two types of chaos. One kind belongs to the Second Law of Thermodynamics, which describes the eventual death of the world as a cup of coffee cooling, never to heat up again. That's bad (degenerative) chaos. It's the chaos writers and artists fear.

But the other type of chaos is hot, turbulent energy—

the far-from-equilibrium state in which order starts breaking out all over. That's good (generative) chaos. It's the productive chaos artists want to know more intimately.

Law operates behind good chaos. I discovered an aspect of this law while watching my own creative experience.

"Writing about" versus "Writing"

Like many novice writers I attempted several approaches to the novel's first blank page. Initially, I assumed the casual attitude of an old cowhand who saunters up to the mare he's been saddling for years: no big deal, just mount the horse and ride the range. I "rode" through three sentences of high mud and turned back. What I need is momentum, I thought. I dashed outside, around the house once, back into the house without slowing down, plopped down at the running computer and handed the baton off to my fingers. They galloped through two paragraphs and then dropped limp. Three more attempts followed. I was discouraged. I thought I knew something about this story. A few characters, some sketchy plot ideas, emerging themes, and a clear sense of the tone of the novel had been floating in mind for several months. But when I typed "Chapter One," it was always the same: no story.

What was I doing wrong? I had disobeyed the cardinal rule of writing a first novel: Never, *never* admit to anyone—especially yourself—that you are writing a novel. Such admission guarantees intimidation and utter terror. I needed an approach that would circumvent the fear. And I discovered one quite by accident.

Minus the courage to plunge into Chapter One, I lapsed into "writing about" the novel. I talked to myself on paper about the characters, their relationships, what we were all learning together. I wrote "something like this" scenes in which I sketched some fog-gray generalities and homed in on a few shining, meaningful sentences. I wrote short vignettes of possible powerful moments and filed them on disk under "epiphs.myb" (epiphanies, maybe). I wrote about plausible themes in long philosophical diversions.

None of this writing was "real"; it was simply possibilities. I was playing around. In the back of my mind these were my process notes. I kept telling myself I needed to know just a little more as my "writing about" spilled over a quarter ream of continuous computer paper.

However, at the same time, I was possessed by frustration over my fear and resistance to writing the novel. In parentheses among story ideas, each day's notes lamented, "What am I doing? Why am I writing all this stuff? WHEN am I going to start the novel?" Soon, abusive comments littered the page: "Come on, you *wimp!* Get your boots on, grab your gun and run into this battle growling!" But I kept "writing about," feeling I needed to know more before I started "real writing."

Quietly, within the lines of "writing about," the story grew. But now I believed that I had already written so much *about* the novel that I had worn myself and the story out. It would never be written. I knew too much to start now. I had done all the work without writing the book. I was sure to have the distinction of being the only writer to record so meticulously the development of an unwritten novel.

Then, one inexplicable day, simultaneously exhausted from "writing about" and tormented by the possible disappointment of never knowing what would happen to these characters I had come to love, I began to write. I learned more by writing the first three paragraphs than I thought I had in months of "writing about."

> They were on the last leg now. As the van reeled through the late night darkness, road signs flared and dissolved under the headlights. Charles mumbled sleepily in the back seat, "Eno elim ot yrref." Morgan and Dad ignored him, as they had for much of the trip.
>
> A week earlier, Charles had taken up the peculiar practice of reading words backward. It had begun at the airport when they were seeing Joan and Bill off.
>
> (Unpublished manuscript)

What? *Who* were Joan and Bill? There was no record of *them* in my "writing about" files. What were they doing here? How could my labored-over story veer out of control in the second paragraph? I snarled but kept going. Two paragraphs later an answer appeared:

> This summer it would be three years since her mother had died. Morgan peered past the dark form of her father sitting beside her. It was Joan who had mothered Morgan these last three years. It was Joan's voice that cheered for Morgan on the sidelines of the hockey field.

At the moment, I was shocked at how such a well-prepared story could take itself off course. I had planned to march straight toward my first epiphany—the first of about three or four power-packed moments in the story. As it happened, Joan and Bill stayed only for three pages, but Joan's relationship with Morgan became the essential background to understanding Morgan's relationship with her father. I was grateful for her interruption.

This small incident shows how writing works. Writing is accretion. It is a plant whose cells reproduce at the tip and push their way through hard ground. The cells are the words and phrases that must "grow" the story relentlessly upward. Annie Dillard describes it this way: "The line of words is a miner's pick, a woodcarver's gouge, a surgeon's probe. You wield it, and it digs a path you follow. Soon you find yourself deep in new territory. Is it a dead end, or have you located the real subject?" (3).

In contrast, "writing about" is random, patchwork growth, not linear accretion. The patchwork quilter works with pieces, first here, then there. The patchwork may be uneven—threadbare rags mingling with precious pieces of handiwork.

When I felt the headstrong power of the "line of words" to chart its own direction, I was dismayed. I thought I would have to throw out the patchwork pieces that seemed to find no coincidence in the line of words. However, I did not then realize that all the preparation of the cursed "writing about" was the root of the plant that would supply the nutrients and support the structure as the tip wormed its way up and out of the dark. It was never a question of either patchwork growth or accretion; it was always both.

Writing is a paradoxical activity. All the methods contradict one another and all the methods complement one another. Every time I pinned down a corner of the writing process, an opposite corner would pop up in rebellion. As soon as I discovered the importance of letting the words lead me to meaning, I was forced into recognizing, as well, the need for knowing meaning before finding the words.

A kind of rhythm vibrates between the opposite corners. Initially, writing seems to require that I know where I am going; yet I learned that writing also requires discovery that can only come from *not* knowing where I am headed. It takes a musician's timing to know the precise moment one should give way to the other. Writing cannot be pinned down into a coherent process except to say that it swings—sometimes wildly, sometimes subtly—between opposing forces. These propel the writing like the inchworm, which contracts in order to expand forward.

In the early stages of writing almost anything, the work is troubled. There is only chaos—for a few hours, a few days, a few weeks. When I was "writing about" the novel, I mistook this as degenerative chaos. The stories would never be written. I thought I was simply avoiding the work. When I tried to write the line of words, I felt at sea and doubtful. I couldn't imagine the story falling into one piece.

The troubling, chaotic periods of creative work usually hover around beginnings. However, in the middle of a story or essay, chaos can reappear and in one short afternoon leave a long wake of destruction. Sometimes I recognize it as a generative chaos, pick up my chin, and keep slogging. Sometimes I give up.

When the wind-spirit moves the waters of the deep, the artist feels first the pleasant and stimulating sense of potential, the conviction that something wonderful hangs just out of reach. She can smell it. It pulls her on to discover its form. But as she reaches to grasp this vision, the spirit troubles the waters into chaos. The joy, assurance, promise, and conviction of potential turn to frustration, doubt, uncertainty. This stage of the creative experience is sometimes protracted, sometimes fleeting. At some point, however, the troubling turns into patterned waves—a balanced tension between opposite forces that propels the work forward.

☙ ☙ ☙

WAVES: CREATIVE TENSION

Writing is so much damned fun. . . . I feel like a kid at
Christmas.   (Tom Clancy in Winokur, 14)

I hate writing. I will do anything to avoid it. The only way
I could write less was if I was dead.
                                    (Fran Lebowitz in Winokur, 15)

Whether the topic is the motivation, process, mission,
or rewards of writing, we can expect contradiction
among writers. However, I was surprised at the quantity
and scope of contradiction within my own writing practice. I had expected mine to be different from the experiences of other writers, but somewhat consistent within
itself.

Writing runs on tension.

Writers and artists understand the value of tension as
a quality in their art—for example, the juxtaposition of
opposite characters, the push-pull of contradictory emotions. Tension produces synergy in the story, poem, or
painting.

And tension works throughout the creative process as
well as within the product. Tension between ways of
working, ways of knowing, ways of being, and ways of
generating ideas move the creative process.

But, like good and bad chaos, two kinds of tension
visit the creative process. Bad tension bogs the work

down. Like Job's devil walking "to and fro on the earth," its energy is all repetitive motion that takes the writing nowhere. But in their early stages, it's often nearly impossible to distinguish good from bad tension.

For instance, the simultaneous abhorrence and need for writing produce a degenerative tension for many writers, including me. Relations of Lebowitz and Clancy live *together* in my head. The result is no writing and a guilty and testy nonwriter going nowhere.

However, I tend to misdiagnose this tension. One day, as I tried to mediate the love/hate battle obstructing my writing, I tripped over the *real* problem, which turned out to be a good tension. It was, I soon discovered, *the* problem of all my creative endeavor.

❦ ❦ ❦

THE FEAR OF FALLING

When the potential—the vision of the work—meets the work itself, tension rises. Of course, they no more meet than heaven and earth. And that is the problem. The vision is something other than the work. We try to hold on to the vision as we turn toward the work we hope will embody that vision. But it begins slipping away even as we take the first glance toward the work. Now we serve two masters, the vision and the work. Both are cheated. By the time the vision falls to earth, it is nothing like the vision.

I am walking homeward beside the fields, when I notice some fluffy white stuff about thirty yards away. It's probably trash, blown from town, or leftovers from the weekend fair. But the windblown trash is too localized and the fields are stripped clean of any evidence of the town celebration. So I walk over to investigate.

As I draw near, I fear it is a dead animal. Closer, I see that the scattered fluffs are downy feathers. I pick them up and marvel at their fineness. They are more like sheer silk than what I think of as a feather. The lump off-center is a gull. Repulsed, but curious, my eye is attracted to the black-and-white tail feathers still deeply anchored to the dead body. Their pattern is striking, like wings of butterflies. I want to pull a couple out to take home.

Squeamish, I focus only on the feather. I pull at it, but it holds firmly. I grasp two feathers, one in each hand, and yank in opposite directions. My eyes and attention are highly focused. I do not think about the bird, the dead body. Only the feathers. I look at them like I look at the contours we draw in art class. The teacher says, "Do not think of the object. Do not *see* an object. See only the lines, the contours. Let your eye trace the line. That is all there is." The two feathers are all there is.

After three pulls, they release their grip. Now I have a bouquet of feathers. I have what I want. But I cannot walk away. I look at the gull. Its body has been ripped open by predators. The claws, once frightful in life, rest like geologic specimens. I turn to my feathers. They're just pieces of matter. I don't have what I want. I don't have graceful, wheeling flight or a pure-white bird plunging into thick, blue sky. I don't have a piece of gull in my hand. It's something else.

The black patterns on the gull's wing are lost in single feathers. It was their placement on the wing that gave the whole its pattern. When they are pulled from the wing, they have no pattern of their own. Later, when I put the bouquet on my desk I will marvel at the beauty and fine workmanship and random black spots. But I will not have a gull.   (Journal)

We cannot tame the vision to a linear procession of words. The work will not be the vision of a gull. But it will be a bouquet of feathers, which isn't bad. Through experience and graceful acceptance this problem can evolve into a good tension that propels the work forward. Rather than ask the potential vision to carry the load, we can let the vision and the work feed each other just as the upward thrust of a wave forms the downward plunge, which in turn impels the next wave.

In good tension, opposing forces provide the traction that sets the creative process in motion.

In 1966 my parents had a turquoise Ford Mustang convertible—a great summer car that turned into a skid-mobile sometime after Christmas in the Michigan winter. At stop signs, snow-drifted ditches lay in ambush as I slowed down just enough to be sucked in. The tires could only spin in the snow. But when I put my dad's steel-mesh "Sno-begone" mats under the tires, the friction propelled me out of the ditch.

Writing is like driving on ice: no friction, no traction. I think it may be the fundamental law behind my writing work.

Tension and Paradox

I had no intimate knowledge of the nature of this tension when I first began to watch my writing process. Prior to formal study of creativity, it had seemed to me that invention was simply making connections—bringing "two" together to synthesize a new "one." Something usually exploded or quietly smoldered when two unrelated things came together. I had developed an active metaphorical sense (relating things and events normally seen as discrete entities), which had grown to the point where it interrupted everyday practical thinking. I was an amateur alchemist haphazardly pitching ideas into the pot: turn up the heat, add a little of this, a little of that. Stand back! If nothing happens, try another combination.

Then, I enlisted in "research and analyze" missions with cognitive psychologists in graduate school. We studied creative processes, heuristics, algorithms, components of creativity, creative personality traits. I practiced taking risks, diverging and converging my thoughts, being more playful, brainstorming, breaking set, keeping options open, being intrinsically rather than extrinsically motivated. In the end, it seemed to me that most techniques still stood in the larger, simpler context of making connections.

I was particularly impressed with the energy excited when two connected ideas were related to a third. Suppose I connect sand and water. I might think how they are alike (grains and drops, waves on the water and wind-swept dunes) or how they are different (warm sand and cool water, dry and wet, smooth and coarse, flowing and stable). But if I connect the two to something else, say, an eye, I come upon more interesting ideas: the water soothes the eye, the sand irritates it; the water reflects light to the eye while the wet, brown sand (I live in New England) absorbs light.

Or suppose I randomly connect "sand" and "water" to "horse." Immediately I think of the way dry sand impedes trotting and how the water's edge makes sand more pleasurable, more supportive, underfoot. I think of how sand kicked up is like and unlike splashes of water; how sand prints remember us, but water leaves no record of our passing. And I think how water receives the swimming horse and buoys him up; how the wet sand does not embrace the horse but supports him so he may go where he wishes without obstruction.

Connections create tension among ideas that attract and repel one another at the same time—ideas that are like and unlike one another. And tension generates more ideas. But I was not consciously aware of the power of paradox—a single idea that curiously includes opposites that appear irreconcilable, thereby tightening the tension. If I look for paradox, I shift into turbotension and increase the power and quality of ideas generated.

Then I will notice that the water *both* soothes (by cooling and cleaning the eye) *and* irritates (by reflecting bright sunlight into the eye); the sand irritates (by scratching the eye) but also soothes (by absorbing the bright sun rays). I will focus on the paradox of the water, which supports and lightens the swimming horse yet controls its movement, and the sand, which does not give like the water yet allows the horse the freedom to run where it wishes.

It is the special tension of paradox that produces interesting, useful ideas. So the greater the opposition within a singular idea, the greater the tension. Yet paradox refers to a "seeming" impossibility. The tension is pleasantly released when the impossibility is resolved. The seeming either/or irreconcilability of tension produced by paradox is fundamental not only to the story but to the processes that create the story. Paradox incites a struggle between opposing forces in order to fall into a deeper peace. Either/or yields on a higher level to both/and. When we quit choosing one or the other and accept both, paradox energy raises thought into a new insight.

Opposites make One. Admittedly, this is no great revelation, but my personal discovery of this conspicuous truth shook *my* world—both my writing and my life. Knowing it intellectually from outside and knowing it intuitively from within were as unlike as watching a made-for-TV earthquake from the couch and actually experiencing the sudden vibration that disconnects muscles from mind and jumbles your inner equilibrium.

Storywriters and poets look through crossed eyes. They must accept their process as an art that is sometimes craft and as a craft that is sometimes art. Nothing about writing is either/or; all of it is both/and. It is tortoise and hare, torture and paradise. It is becoming one with the cosmos before dinner only to have it to crumble into chaos by bedtime. It is the humble seeker, silently praying to know the path, as well as the macho cowboy, whooping and whipping the herd onto the trail. It is the single, inspired idea redeeming life—the unexpected prince who chooses you as his only dance partner—but it is also being propositioned by legions of low-potential ideas and having to sell your soul to grab hold of just one.

Once I recognized it, the tension of paradox appeared not just in using connections to generate ideas but throughout the spectrum of creative process—stretching from the immediate stages in which words and meaning pound each other into sentences to the hidden processes in which the writer's opposing attitudes and qualities motivate the writing and contrary ways of knowing and working push the work forward.

❦ ❦ ❦

WAYS OF KNOWING
Reason and Intuition

"Intuition" is a word open to a wide spectrum of meaning. Definitions range from "hunches that are wrong most of the time" (by skeptical rationalists) to "the knowledge of God" (by sympathetic philosophers). Certainly, the word inclines toward faith and subjectivity and away from empiricism and objectivity. But because of its broad translation, it is often bent and stretched to mean whatever the user wishes—which I suppose is appropriate given its inclination toward subjectivity. Language needs elasticity as well as precision. But, talking about intuition on any but the broadest terms subjects meaning to confusion and controversy.

In her book *Awakening Intuition,* Frances Vaughan explains that while intuition appears to conflict with reason, more often "it is simply outside the ways of knowing that depend on ordinary sensory channels for information." She refers to intuition as a way of knowing that transcends the separation between subject and object—the knower becomes one with the known and "knows from the inside."

My own affinity for intuition became apparent when I noticed how often I erupted at the rationalist, pseudo-scientific, how-to explanations of creativity by cognitive psychologists. Naturally, a writer or artist who disdains intuition (I've never met one) would characterize the elements and processes of creation differently than I. I am coming at the creative process from the direction of intuition because it is basic to my personal process and is therefore important for me to know more deeply. And, of course, while I recognize that every area of life demonstrates creativity, I am looking at creativity in the context of art and writing. Viewed from other contexts the findings will differ.

All this is not to say that we should slight reason of its role in creative expression. Intuition inspires a work of art and then guides the artist to its fulfillment. While it generally works alone in inspiration, it must join with reason to execute the creative product. Recognizing the power of intuition does not sacrifice reason but balances it for higher, more-efficient flight.

Early on, I found I could best understand my personal creativity in terms of intuition and could understand intuition most directly as the opposite of rational thinking. (This is because, like most, my education was founded on the "rock" of rational modes instead of the "fluff" of intuition.)

Rather than analyze intuition, I chose simply to take in its feeling. First I noticed the "high" that intuition gave me through inspiration and insight and the sense of potential discovery. Then I recognized that no matter the form of inspiration, I felt its significance and power before I knew its meaning or identity. This struck me as a direct opposite of reason.

I could command reasoning; I had no such authority over intuition. Reason seemed active, while intuition appeared more passive—I manufactured reasoned concepts, but I received intuitions.

Reason impressed me by its *known* meaning. Intuition impressed me by its *promised* meaning. Reason required proof, while intuition depended on a sense of rightness, appropriateness.

I judged reason by its steplike process according to learned rules. I judged intuition by its sheer power, its push on my consciousness. (Sometimes this was an explosive push, as in inspiration; other times it was a persistent pressure guiding me forward in the work.)

Intuition felt like play; rational thinking was work. Rational thinking functioned better the harder I concentrated. Intuition happened when I let go.

Reason worked by way of doubt, dialectic; intuition worked through empathy, acceptance. Intuition perceived what was hidden, before it had been tested, verified, and articulated by reason.

Reason might be of the head, but intuition often involved my whole being. Sometimes my stomach felt an intuition before I was conscious of it.

The languages of intuition were separate and distinct from the languages of reason. Reasoning typically employed words, symbols, equations, and signs. However, intuition spoke—albeit with conviction and authority—in images and cinematic scenes, strong feelings, moods and tones of mind, musical sounds and phrases.

The more I observed intuition the more I became convinced its languages were infinite. These languages are what Jung calls "the deep presentiments that strive to find expression" (164). They are much more than hunches or vague feelings; they are powerful, compelling convictions.

Probably my strongest motive for writing is the "high" of intuition's inspiration and insight. And this feeling is a release that is most pleasing against a background of effortful, rational work. Intuition and reason work together, back and forth, giving and taking. Intuition sees powerfully, ahead of reason; but reason defines the form. This is the traction between two opposite ways of knowing that moves the work forward.

Once I perceived the distinctions between rational thinking and intuition, once their delineations rose in bas-relief in my consciousness, I was prepared to see them as one.

Opposite ways of knowing need each other. By attempting to synthesize these two ways of knowing into one, or by ignoring the distinct contribution of intuition, creativity theorists would lose the good tension that propels the work. Surely scientists as well as artists demonstrate this to be true. Both physicist Fritjof Capra and research psychologist Lawrence Le Shan spotlight the similarity of worldviews held by modern physicists and mystics. Capra argues for a dynamic interplay, rather than a synthesis, between mystical intuition and scientific analysis. Le Shan says these two different ways of knowing need to be integrated in our lives "so that each viewpoint is heightened and sharpened by the knowledge of the other" (100).

Art and its creation deal in paradox. Ha! *Life* deals in paradox. If we wish to transcend and resolve it, we need to learn to play with opposites—not merely put up with them. We need to embrace them as "both and oneful" (e.e. cummings).

So I must be mindful not to disdain reason. Vaughan, acknowledging the necessity and power of rational thinking, offers good counsel to creativity theorists and artists alike when she warns, "Let the mind be guided by reason, not bound by it" (177).

Trusting Heart to Mind, Mind in Heart

During the early stages of "writing about" my novel, I couldn't accept this activity as "real," productive writing. I was pretending to be a writer. I felt guilty. Why? Because I had heard and read too often how most writers jump into their work *writing;* they don't pussyfoot around the pool by writing *about* their work. E. L. Doctorow says, "Planning to write is not writing. Outlining a book is not writing. Researching is not writing. Talking to people about what you're doing, none of that is writing. Writing is writing" (in Winokur, 15).

My torment was how to dethrone this tentative "writing about" and instate real writing. I knew the culprits, to be sure: avoidance and cowardice. But more important, underneath these villains lay a dangerous fear of what words might do to my ideas and emotions, which felt so comfortable unformed in the womb.

I was living with my story on an abstract plane. I entered into the tone, lived vague scenes of great emotional impact, and entertained characters who had no flesh and blood. These feelings gave me joy and satisfaction. But I was living in the fullness of a *potential*, an ideal. The expectations for such inspired moments are huge. Their translation from heaven to earth, from pure inspiration to form, always loses something. The temptation is to accept an unending period of gestation, never to bring to birth, because of the pain of parturition:

> I am afraid to write. I am afraid to give birth to a mortal thing and lose the divine idea. I cannot have both. If the divine comes to earth in flesh and blood, in time and space, it will lose its divinity. But it is that divinity—that unformed potential—that fills me with such energy. (Process notes)

I had to learn to commit my deepest experiences and feelings to the limitations of specific words rather than write *around* these experiences using temporary, less definite language. Although I was writing, my focus was still on the ephemeral emotions; the focus had to shift to the writing. Vapory, floating inspiration must condense into the vessel of words. Form has its own beauty and joy, distinct from its original impetus but still connected to it. For the writer, the right words can later cue the original inspiration, bring back its fullness. But we cannot expect words to *embody* that fullness for others.

I had to see that the inspiration of awe and the energy of potential would never write the novel. Original inspiration must be transformed from passive experience to brick-solid meaning through active work. The writer must move from heart (the passionate yet vague sense of potential) to mind (the detailed work of discovering, constructing, and articulating meaning).

For there to be art, the heart must trust the mind's words and not fear the deflation that comes when words cannot express the full inspiration. My "writing about" had to yield to the line of words that worked out meaning and story in a different way.

I had to learn anew the old relationship between inspiration (the heart's experience) and perspiration (the mind's search for words). It is the rhythm of two mountaineers with a life rope between them: first one climbs, gains a sure foot, then supports the other's ascent. Sometimes I am impelled to write by inspiration; other times I have to write for pages in order to become inspired.

However, the responsibilities of heart and mind, inspiration and intellect, are often blurred. There seem to be no rules, at least in my process. Whether to let the heart lead or the mind, intuition or reason, is a decision left, in the end, to "feel."

Robert Henri says that passion must continue during the work of creation:

> . . . it is not enough to have thought great things *before* doing the work. The brush stroke at the moment of contact carries inevitably the exact state of being of the artist at that exact moment into the work . (16–17)

However, as usual, there is paradox and contradiction. Madeleine L'Engle agrees with Henri that passion, or "heat," is necessary, but she cautions against it during creative work:

> Tremendous heat is needed in generating [poetry], but during the actual "making" there must be ice. . . . All the scenes that move me deeply while I am writing them end up in the wastepaper basket. (53)

L'Engle and Henri do not disagree. I don't believe L'Engle is advising us to give up "heat"; rather, she wants us to add "ice" for counterpoint. Passion and intellect, heat and ice—they are "both and oneful."

Somewhere in the creative experience the two feuding parts of ourselves make peace. Heart and mind, intellect and intuition, hot passion and cool reason, work off each other toward a single destination.

But however evenly the heart-intellect balance might alternate at the chapter and page levels, the overarching balance in the work as a whole is clear to me. I must work with mind in heart rather than with heart in mind. To write stories that bring home views beyond the realm of intellect I need intellect as a tool. Intellect may carry the baggage and help intuition to find the way, but it cannot take in the views glimpsed by intuition.

❦ ❦ ❦

WAYS OF BEING

A Rich Life versus "Monotonous Days"

> Writers don't have lifestyles. They sit in little rooms and write. (Norman Mailer in Winokur, 17)

Ten years ago, I took a lingering look at the people whose lives I admired most. They were active, rich, and thoughtful: world-traveling anthropologists who allowed the yeast of foreign cultures to leaven their lives; artists who through uncommon discipline had chiseled precise grooves in their early years and were now broadening those grooves into wider paths, reaching beyond themselves and their art; multidisciplined (some would say unfocused) women who used art and craft to do good in extraordinary and unexpected environments. These people had managed to pull together the diversity of life with exuberant activity and clearheaded awareness. They were thoughtful learners of life, not hovering analysts. When I counted them, I noticed only one writer. My own had not yet become a writing life, because I feared an early death by writing. I was too young to live my days as an observer at a desk. Life was for the living. So I wrote only on the edge of life, at day's end.

Once, however, I caught myself writing under my breath during a walk. I was struggling to describe the air, to pinpoint the essence of its particular feel and scent that day. Suddenly I thought, How long have I been doing this? Surprised, I recognized it as habitual behavior. I did not know when it had started, but after that walk I discovered I was doing it nearly all the time I was alone. I also realized that I played with metaphor like one of those irksome punsters who cannot stop themselves at parties. And I found myself frequently lost in short dialogues between fictitious other people and myself. I was discovering an underside to my outer life—the writing side.

In retrospect I can identify those playful habits as a way to appreciate life by working out meaning. I was straining to catch life's breath, to fill the depth of some cavity. Eventually, writing in my head spilled over onto scraps of paper in the middle of the day. Much later I came to accept as true for myself Anne Morrow Lindbergh's words: "I must write. . . . For writing is more than living, it is being conscious of living" (in Calkins, 3). I suppose this is why many artists paint, dancers dance, musicians compose, and comedians invent comic routines.

Because of writing I am more susceptible to life. My senses are clearer, my compassion more acute, my tolerance wider, my love and gratitude deeper. My grandmother was a painter who saw paintings everywhere. Storytellers and writers see stories all around them. It is the way people see that is the substance of their life.

Whenever I become impatient with the dullness of days of writing, I think of Annie Dillard's words:

> There is no shortage of good days. It is good lives that are hard to come by. A life of good days lived in the senses is not enough. The life of sensation is the life of greed; it requires more and more. The life of the spirit requires less and less; time is ample and its passage sweet. . . . A day that closely resembles every other day of the past ten or twenty years does not suggest itself as a good [life]. But who would not call Pasteur's life a good one, or Thomas Mann's? (32–33)

So, what of my life behind the desk? Baudelaire's maxim "monotonous days, exciting literature" (in Sweeney, 11) is certainly no comfort. Yes, there are monotonous days. And, yes, I am tempted again to try the old terry-robe sash. The blandness of a string of writing days can still trigger my "get real and get a life" reflex. But those days are balanced by a life made rich under the writer's lens—the way of seeing that intensifies, clarifies, and expands everyday life and allows me to live more fully than before I wrote.

At times I am sure this is the right life. I let space and time swallow me. I am alone, available to an undiscovered universe. I resent unexpected interruption.

But then Diana, a longtime friend, bursts into my life again. Diana with the life that spills all over the edges so I cannot tell where her life ends and the world begins. A day with her, and I shun my quiet life of thoughts and words.

I'm a switch-hitter. It depends on what's being pitched at me. The question of whether I should write or have a full life no longer itches my peace of mind. More often now, the wind's troubling falls into gentle waves because I'm more alert to the either/or trap. When one day I long for the profound, spiritual life that yields insights for healing the world's stresses and pains and a few days later I am sure that my true calling is to choreograph concert stage shows in Rome to raise money for the homeless, I don't agonize in repression or frustration. Now I laugh.

These contradictory pulls are not the wild thrashings they seem. They're more like an exaggerated dream trying to tell me something from a neglected corner of the psyche: "Your life is becalmed in the doldrums of either/or." I need wind and waves—a little inspiration and some tension. It's a call for a gentle acceptance of an opposite way of being to balance and energize my present way.

The tension between monotonous days and a rich life incites a rhythm that moves the work and the life.

Making? Or Taking What Comes?

This is the big one: should I take more control of my life or should I respond to it, adapt to it? Discontentment always brings this question to the surface. It consistently presents itself as a choice between the two. I know people who carry life lists around and check the items off regularly. They are making a life. I know other people whose moments flow naturally one into the next. They take life as it comes, welcoming rather than fighting inner changes.

But like most of us, I suspect, I can't choose. I find myself at crossroads, vacillating between two extremes and feeling bad about it. Should I let my life change me, or should I change my life? While I try to resolve the philosophical debate, I go nowhere.

For me, the question will never be resolved. I must grow beyond the question rather than force an answer. This is typical of the paradoxes of life and art, which are resolved by rising above the dilemma rather than battling it out on the level of either/or, which of two. That's what paradoxes do: they lift us and force us to grow. Which one? is the wrong question.

A river runs through the cavity of the land. It bends in peaceful submission to the land's topography, churns over rocks, fills a placid pool of stones, throws itself off cliffs in grandeur and abandon. The land makes the river.

But the river also carves and deepens the land it follows. It changes course, wearing down the very rock that shaped it and the stones that obstructed it. It nourishes the land that holds it. Fed by the river's nutrients and water, vegetation enriches the soil, stabilizes the land, and protects it from erosion. The river makes the land.

The land and the river are "both and oneful." And so it is with making life and taking life as it comes. I inhale. I exhale. They are of one breath. Making and taking are of one spirit. I am not torn between dualities, walking to and fro like Job's devil, arriving nowhere. The spirit I inhale (my taking—acceptance, response, and adaptation to all that life gives) and the spirit I exhale (what I purposefully make of life) are one spirit.

Outside and inside are one (but not the same). A rhythm swings within this oneness—between making and taking, following and leading, a radiant vision and a shadowy trust. And this rhythm musters a wave to propel life forward.

Of course, the rhythm will wobble. Disturbed cadences and cycles will trouble the water. I will fall into the familiar limbo of the awful duality. Which one? I will ask. Which way?

How do we regain that rhythm? We don't. Whatever skews the rhythm is telling us it's time to find, to fall into, a new pattern. And this new pattern is simply a higher order of the oneness of life's making and taking. The agony of choice will, once again, resolve into the grace that includes both.

Giving In to the Opposites in Good Tension

we are so both and oneful
night cannot be so sky
sky cannot be so sunful
i am through you so i   (e.e. cummings)

One difficulty with the tension between ways of being is the narrow-mindedness of believing we are either "this" or "that." Arguments pop up every day: hard-nosed, bottom-line real estate tycoons *cannot* be sympathetic community volunteers. An intelligent protector-of-the-downtrodden journalist cannot be a patient bureaucrat. We say this is the nature of the personality. We accept that if a person is a planner, she cannot be a dreamer. If he's a reformer, he can't be a follower. If she's a creative, spontaneous homemaker, she can't possibly be a tax specialist. People inhabit hard-edged boxes. We like them that way. On the bad side, we severely limit each other. On the good side, such reasoning allows us to complement and help one another rather than live like islands.

However, here we are speaking of qualities that transcend personal natures and inclinations, qualities that balance individual lives and work. No matter what the job, economy must balance spending. The journalist, with free words at his disposal, uses them carefully. He knows there is a time for bare-bones writing and a time for Louis XIV flamboyance. Accountants and storytellers live together inside journalists.

The novelist must be an observer and a manipulator. She watches her characters develop on their own as well as manipulates them into their proper places; she is audience as well as director, appreciative as well as demanding. (Nabokov said he treated his characters like galley slaves. John Fowles said he put the French lieutenant's woman on the balcony to jump, but she wouldn't.)

I need a generous hospitality to the diverse ways of being that would take up residence within my psyche.

Continuity loses its definition without change. Stability without flexibility turns into rigidity. Care unpartnered by faith withers into fear. Spontaneity unbalanced by responsibility spins out of orbit into impulsiveness. "i am through you so i." The leader through becoming a follower is more a leader; freedom through the lens of discipline is more freedom; joy through the experience of sorrow is more joy.

I must first perceive the dynamic balance of the spirit that moves over the waters of the soul. Then I must trust myself to the breath of that spirit. And let myself be breathed. The needed balance is not gained by compromising opposite qualities and living somewhere in the middle but by swinging the full arc between opposites and taking joy in the spirited tension that enriches and moves life.

❧ ❧ ❧

WAYS OF WORKING

Tortoise and Hare

When I finally surrendered to the line of words, I felt its keen senses sniff, squint, and deliberately grope toward the story inch by inch. The straight, one-dimensional line struck me as a separate animal from the frivolous, unfocused, loose, and vague "writing about." "At last," I said, "I'm writing mean and lean." I rejected the amateurish "writing about" as an ineffective hare who jumped here and there, forward and back, and never finished the race.

However, weak moments brought relapses of hare writing. I told myself it was to be expected in breaking such a tyrannical habit. Then, at a particularly low point in my self-esteem, I caught something out of the corner of my eye. Something good was going on between the two modes of writing. A rhythm between "writing about" and the line of words was finding its beat. The writing began to breathe—inhaling, exhaling. My novel was a slippery road, but "writing about" and the line of words pressed against each other to give me some traction.

Hare and tortoise, no longer competitors, became a relay team. Together they would win the race. In this sense, Doctorow is wrong. I could not separate the planning, researching, and daydreaming that occurred while "writing about" from "writing." Toni Morrison says, "I type in one place, but I write all over the house" (in Winokur, 129).

The productive tension between the line of words and the expanding patchwork of "writing about" represents the whole (the larger picture, the broad themes) working against the part (the smaller picture, the more specific events). It includes the unforeseen balancing the foreseen. During creative work, the character of this tension continually takes new but related forms: the oscillation between analysis and synthesis, convergence and divergence, contraction and expansion, construction and discovery. There are cycles of controlling and letting go, intervals of coming together and falling apart.

The Foreseen and the Unforeseen

Before he had picked up a single tool, Michelangelo envisioned in its entirety the form of "David" in a fourteen-foot block of stone; the sculptor had only to remove the excess (Finlayson, 10). He worked from without, chipping away the false to uncover the true.

Conversely, Mihaly Csikszentmihalyi, a psychologist who studies creativity, discovered that artists produced paintings far removed from their original concept because the painters engaged discovery, risked new paths during the creation of their work, and thereby came upon final forms never envisioned at the inception (208).

Not only are both creative processes valid, but they support one another.

The tireless line of words that nudged its way into the unknown worked in counterpoint to the fitful "writing about" that jumped ahead into the unknown in order to scout out possible routes. Discovery and surprise balanced expectation and design. Knowing and not knowing where I was headed were equally valuable.

I found that a story can grow outward toward unforeseen form. The line of words slowly exudes a soft substance that will harden into new ground. But just as often, form is glimpsed before thought or words expand into its expression, as in Michelangelo's experience with "David."

With the popularity of "process writing" many teachers advise students to "free write" and then revise, revise, revise. The theory is twofold: one, that by taking attention off words writers will stumble onto meaning; and two, that getting the "whole" down and then revising is more efficient than a rambling writing process.

"Process writing" is prejudiced against the line of words. Often I cannot progress without perfecting each word and phrase. At such times the words become fine chisels that patiently pick along the rich veins in order to bring out the story's delicate details. Stories find themselves in the particulars, in the well defined.

But at other moments I have to release my grip on fine words and details and swing broadly with a machete through the dense potential of story ideas that crowd my way. Then the writing is quick and the revisions are many. Often we need a rough-cut path before we can turn back and search out the details that give interest and meaning to creative expression.

When I know the direction of the story, I must wrestle words to that ground and pin them there, train them to a trellis of foreseen meaning. At other times I feel compelled to allow words the freedom to wander as they may. Then words lead to new meaning.

However, the story's integrity must ever supervise the words. Words may begin as trustworthy guides through untrod territories only to turn into drunken explorers with no destination. If the focus remains on the story, the words will be genuine and appropriate. They will further the story along its course—foreseen or unforeseen. But if the focus shifts to the words—their beauty, wit, impressiveness, or taut shape—the words will betray the story. I felt I did my best writing when I rappelled along the cliff's edge, clinging to the rock wall of the story while yet enjoying the short flights of free descent that words offered.

Writing, like all art, requires nimbleness. Anyone who has studied jazz dance knows what I mean. Sudden changes in direction and balance can render graceful bodies clumsy and tentative. Just so, the constant shifts in creative tension require at once flexibility and control. Bach addicts love counterpoint—two separate lines of music each managing to keep its distinct identity while creating a harmonic relationship with the other. When we can hear three—the two lines and the new thing created between them—we know how creative tension feels.

Cosmos and Chaos: Falling Apart versus Coming Together

Cosmos is the reason I write. I want to see the world as one, connected, interrelated. That interconnectedness is meaning. Writing helps me, forces me, to see and affirm meaning. But this wholeness is glimpsed in time as a continual unfolding that changes and renews. And the path to renewal is to fall apart.

In my early days of writing I would be euphoric with a vision of the whole, thinking "I've got it! I know where all this is going." Then, it would fall apart as I continued writing and I would be depressed, thinking "I've lost it somewhere" or "I was wrong—that wasn't really the story." The experience held a sense of failure and impatience as though the process consisted of first finding the right goal and then proceeding toward it.

Sometime later I realized what storywriting is. It is a self-correcting guided missile aimed at a moving target. In order to write I must be guided by a vision of the whole. But as I write, the words influence my vision of the whole through new discovery. The whole no longer works as a guiding vision. It is somehow off the mark. It falls apart (it takes only a moment), and from its fragments another whole vision begins to form. While walking one day I saw migrating geese imitating the writing process:

> They lift in a terrible chaos of honking and wing beating, tilting bodies all askew. Eventually they assemble into a perfect V formation and slice effortlessly through the thin, clear air with muffled voice. But when it comes time to land, they break formation, collapse in a honking dither and pummel the earth with crash landings. (Process notes)

In the early stages of writing stories, the vision of the whole is vague. As it continually falls apart and re-forms, it gains definition. Often writers do not see the whole clearly until the book is finished. (Near the end of his life, Schopenhauer noticed in looking back that his life contained an order much like a composed novel. He pointed out that life had a self-structuring quality that could only be perceived as a whole from the vantage of old age [Maher, 24].)

So cosmos and chaos are partners, but not equal

partners. Just as I feel I must work with mind in heart, so I must work with chaos in cosmos. The attention is on cosmos. Chaos serves cosmos. Chaos comes to lift me to a higher, more comprehensive cosmos.

And, as always, there are exceptions. Sometimes the best writing is not the result of any struggle, of cosmos repeatedly falling into chaos. The words are so aligned with the inspiration that the writing flows without effort. The inspiration is utterly clear. Perhaps the vision needs no re-forming. Such writing is without the weight of process. It is the writing I long for but never can predict.

Controlling and Letting Go

In school, I viewed writing as the quintessence of control. Only people who could control their thoughts—collect them, relate them, organize them, store them, and then apply them appropriately—were candidates for the office of Writer. School approached the subject of writing as a two-step march: first, think very clearly in terms of an outline—good outline, good thinking; second, write from the outline—I. ABC, II. ABC . . . Aspiring writers adeptly picked their way through heaps of vocabulary lists, punctuation drills, literature analyses, sentence diagrams, and academic papers—the required obstacle course leading to language facility.

Writing was separate, in my mind, from storytelling, which called for skills from another planet: imagination, style, joy and pathos, wisdom, and a certain looseness. This looseness included freedom, lack of inhibition, a willingness to take risks—an all-out letting go. In school the writer was a controlled technician, the storyteller a spontaneous artist. And I was neither.

Much later, I wanted both.

> Alright, now everyone's switching to the organic, developmental writing method. As I understand it, I'm just supposed to write and write and write and write and somehow my thoughts will begin to organize themselves. (Journal)

Early work in process writing had the smell of chaos theory, of troubled waters falling into patterned waves. E. M. Forster summed it up when he said, "How do I know what I think until I see what I write?" (in Winokur, 20).

Under this new regime, I began to write with abandon, not caring so much what came out on paper. Mostly I used this technique when I was unsure what I really wished to say—in other words, a good portion of the time. It was talking through the problem on paper. It was successful.

I noticed that these writing spells were generating reams of *other stuff* on the side. Stuff having no relation to the writing at hand. Interesting stuff. I tracked it along its labyrinthine course and discovered all kinds of interesting other material. Writing was FUN! Soon I was exploring more than expounding. Discovery was the name of the game. My bread-and-butter professional writing work looked bleak by comparison. Off with the heels and straight skirt! On with the khaki shorts and hiking boots!

One day, however, I recognized I could not be a purist.

I don't get stuck in process (developmental) writing. That is the problem. I don't stop. I'm a ball of unwinding string, a late-night, run-at-the-mouth radio talk show host. Although novel discoveries occur, the ideas need a rest to get their bearings, coalesce, find structure. I see that multidimensional thought is better suited than linear writing to organizing—seeing the big picture, context, and relationships. For this, more happens on walks than at the desk.   (Process notes)

Thereafter I fell into a natural and irregular alternation between herding thoughts into a line of words and putting them out to pasture where I could watch them mingle. Developmental writing gets the juices flowing, jump-starts thinking. But thinking it over rationally/consciously and mulling it over intuitively/subconsciously must follow.

This sometimes works like an easy party of your favorite friends. You know each of them on many different levels. You watch them interact one-on-one and in groups. You see the multiplicity of their personalities in diverse contexts. The possibilities in your tiny living room are infinite.

But other times, it takes place in a hostile courtroom in which sensitive parties state their case and refuse to give way, all the while straining at bits of truth.

The oscillating action of controlling/letting go, writing about it/thinking about it, works throughout the process, from the early intuitions to final revision.

Ray Bradbury counsels fiction writers with the words "Don't Think!" His path to "Don't Think!" is "Work" and "Relax":

> The artist must work so hard, so long, that a brain develops and lives, all of itself, in his fingers. . . . Work then, hard work, prepares the way for the first states of relaxation. . . . As in learning to typewrite, a day comes when the single letters asdf and jkl; give way to a flow of words. . . . Not to work is to cease, tighten up, become nervous, and therefore destructive of the creative process. . . . WORK RELAXATION DON'T THINK . . . if one works, one finally relaxes and stops thinking. True creation occurs then and only then.
>
> (117–31)

If you cannot control your controlling instincts, take up gardening. But be careful. A lot of writers give up writing for gardening.

> The garden catalogs come in January. I dog-ear their pages. I highlight short, medium, and tall perennials, vines and climbing roses, ground covers, small flowering trees, until most of the print turns yellow. Then I make lists. Then rough plans. Soon I am buying graph paper at Wal-Mart. By April, I phone in my orders. We're talking days of hours of work here. Then something happens between April and June. I forget about

the elaborate designs. When the plants arrive sporadically in June, I act as though there has been no winter of planning. At first, I think I'll just stick the stock in the ground to hold them for "real" planting. But soon I am using some judgment, some aesthetic sense. I plant with no regard for the graph paper, the culture lists, the planting directions. Suddenly, I can picture the sky-blue salvia among the orange enchantment lilies. I will only put in a couple. But I get muddy before changing my clothes or shoes. Then I move the papavers next to the iris. I notice how last fall's blazing pink monarda accidently landed next to the red species. I decide they belong together no matter what the garden books say. Now it begins. I see the beauty of the garden. Not the paper garden I have planned and made, but the garden that is unfolding before my eyes and under my broken nails. I am a partner with the garden. This year's paper designs will be filed with all the rest for another time. But they will never become real gardens, because that's not how gardens are made.

(Journal)

Writing is not more cerebral than gardening. It is doing more than planning. It is responding to beauty, to insight, to pattern, to surprise.

For me the control/let go paradox is resolved in this: I must use the growing control of words and techniques (gained through disciplined practice) to serve the letting go. Controlling must be held in the context of letting go, like mind in heart and chaos in cosmos.

But a more profound sense of letting go continues to hound me. I know my joy in the high of inspiration, intuition, insight: I want to ride the waves, not make them. I want to let go, to let something larger control me. Polly Berrien Berends came close to describing the sense of it:

> On the surface it seems that the music is produced by the power of the conductor to tell everyone what to do and when to do it. He may have to do that, but it is not what makes the music. A good conductor . . . is primarily a listening individual: even while the orchestra is performing loudly he is listening inwardly to silent music. He is not so much commanding as he is obedient. The conductor conducts by being conducted. He first hears, feels, loses himself in the silent music; then when he knows what it is, he finds a way to help others hear it too. He knows that music is not made by people playing instruments, but rather by music playing people. . . . The conductor knows that music makes the music. (160)

But *what* am I letting go? The me that wants to control or fears not to control. My self. Ego.

I can recognize ego taking the reins when the words become more important than honesty. It happens suddenly. I will begin a sentence with one thought and then stumble onto some impressive words that grab attention. The words might sound important, clever, or just particularly clear. They make me want to make waves. Or the words might sound full of potential and truth. They make we want to ride the waves. If it's potential I hear, I follow. If it's cleverness or self-inflation, I dive for the backspace key. It has to do with listening, and I speak to that in the next chapter.

❦ THREE ❦

Fire

Lightning cracks open
the black bowl of sky.
The earth rolls
and dayfire inflames its rim.   (Journal)

When high-tension electrical energy discharges in the atmosphere, it strikes through the night with sudden and surprising fire. But the fire of dawn leaks slowly, washing the earth in daylight.

Ideas strike; ideas dawn. They appear as fierce, concentrated light or as gentle, dispersed light.

Focus gathers light—ideas—into creative expression. Of all the tools of creation, focus is fundamental. Generally, in recollection as well as during creative work, I noticed my attention conformed to the concentrated and the dispersed modes of light—assuming two styles of focus.

On the one hand, my focus was narrow and concentrated. A laser beam, like lightning, is intense light energy. Unlike normal light, which has varying wavelengths, laser light consists of waves the same length. When all the energy is concentrated at the same wavelength, it produces a piercing, powerful beam. Writing focus is as concentrated as a laser.

Just as often, however, my attention was loose, dispersed. A satellite moves in an unobstructed orbit high above earth in order to receive information in many different forms from disparate sources. The writer's attention is like a gigantic satellite—wide open, waiting, and ready to gather incoming signals of varied wavelengths from all directions, which it must then sort, amplify, and translate.

These two breeds of focus join with all the other good tensions in the oscillating, vibrating motion of creation.

❧ ❧ ❧

THE VOICE OF THE STORY AND TRUTH

When I first observed the conceptual stages of my novel, I was busy trying to be creative, to entertain a multiplicity of ideas, to stretch my mind beyond the ideas that came easily. I tried SCAMPER techniques (Separate, Combine, Adapt, Magnify/Minify, Put to other uses, Eliminate, Reverse) (Gallo) and forced relationships and several other methods for generating ideas. They worked in that the ideas were many; but they failed in that too few ideas were useful or appropriate. Two experiences illustrate what I mean.

After a couple of months thinking about the novel and writing notes, I realized I was filtering my entire life through the eyes of the story. Everyone I met held some key to one of my characters; every event in my life gave some insight into the plot. While my observational skills were certainly heightened by this neurosis, the novel was traveling toward no particular point—especially not a climax. I was constantly searching for more interesting ideas. Finally, there came the moment of realization: I had to STOP thinking of ideas. My problem was not ideas. My problem was how to know which were the *right* ideas.

At another time, I was blocked, without ideas, and decided to try the old combination approach. Two stories were occupying the back rooms of my mind: one about a carousel and another about a motley group of house painters known as the Infinity Painting Company. Put together, they became a story about a carousel renovation conducted by some spicy characters. I felt potential in it (and still do). However, the marriage produced too many wayward children, who trampled my original carousel story into a disheveled heap. There was nothing to do but annul the union and start over. While the combination technique worked by suggesting another interesting story, it actually diverted me from an unseen path that was shaping the original story.

After some time spent applying such techniques and trying to embody creative personality traits, I realized I was circling the track in an endless "Creativity 500" whose only purpose was to invent more ideas faster. The point was not the generation of many ideas or even original ideas; what I felt I needed were *appropriate* ideas.

"Appropriate to what?"

"To the story."

"What story? There *is* no story. That's why I need these ideas!"

And so began lesson number one: there *is* a story and I must be quiet, respectful, and utterly faithful in listening for the ideas that will unfold it. If I am in the noisy business of trying to generate droves of creative ideas, I will miss the essential ones.

I have heard of sheep in the Middle East who know their shepherd's voice so well that in a crowded pen of many flocks and many voices they hear only their own shepherd and follow his voice without confusion. In the beginning I did not know the voice of my story nor even that it had one. So I roamed the teeming marketplace of ideas, looking for possibilities.

But the realm of possibilities is seductive in its vastness, like a tidal sea pulling away from shore. It is easy to be lost in the depths when there is no voice calling. The voice guides through the throng of ideas and leads to the appropriate ones.

So *what* is this voice? *Whose* is it? Many of my notes

spoke directly to or indirectly about this voice, but never did I try to lure the voice from its natural mystery into cold daylight for research purposes.

I'm writing round and round—not with the precision of an eagle who circles in on her prey. More like the buzzing bee who's looking for the better nectar haphazardly. I can smell it . . . I know it's somewhere—whoops, HERE, HERE it is! Gee, it's so clear when I've hit it. There's no vagueness to it. THIS is it!

If I am the creator of this story, then it exists only in my mind when my mental actions conceive it. I am the director of this film. So WHO am I talking to, consulting with? Why do I feel there is a dialogue here? Worse, why do I get ANSWERS? Am I a split personality talking to myself—one of my many selves? I can't handle that right now. I get squirrelly if I start thinking of myself as a fragmented being—a broken mirror's reflection of something whole. I feel a whole lot better knowing that there is a story—separate from me—that's simply using me to be born—yes, I'm a midwife. What's saner than that?

O.K. You WIN. I know, I know, you always do. I pushed and shoved to keep that passage in Chapter Two. I begged, Come on, I LOVE that passage. But NO, you say, it doesn't fit. Well, I'd like to know, WHY doesn't it fit? Looks perfectly good to ME. And all you say to me is I'll understand later. And I have to listen. Sometimes you're a gentle spirit, sometimes you're a boot-camp commander.

Am beginning to understand how to follow intuition a little better. I can't be ornery. She needs respect—or should I say I need to respect her in order to understand better—no, to HEAR better. I have to plan on being obedient to intuition, to that little voice. No fair asking for advice and then saying, well it wasn't the greatest advice, I'll do something else. I'm coming to realize that listening includes the promise to obey what I hear. Boy, does that sound like a totalitarian dictator or what? But it's not like that. There is love . . . and trust. If I trust in the wisdom of this voice, I'm not afraid to follow it. If I love it, I will hear it. The inclination to listen AND MEAN IT (be obedient) seems to make for better leading, sharper hearing. I don't claim to understand this stuff. I'm just tellin' it like it is.

At first the voice was all mumbles. But as I've listened, it's become sharper. Because I'm still writing my story I don't want even to whisper the question, "Well, who IS this voice?" I just know it's the voice of the story leading me. I trust it—and not without reason.

(Process notes)

The reason for that day's trust was a particular passage in the story that appeared to write itself. In the first chapter Morgan remembers,

When she was four or five, she had believed her father when he told her the secret of the Big Dipper. Climbing into his lap on the porch swing, she had looked along his arm as it stretched out and up. At the end of his finger hung the cup of the Big Dipper. He had explained that the cup was there to catch falling stars. Then, when it was full—usually late on a August night—it tilted and poured the stars toward Earth.

She had kept this secret faithfully. Whenever the Dipper moved within view of her bedroom window, she had knelt in the dark stillness, watching and waiting. She had imagined how the silent, cool star-shower would spill down and flicker like fireflies scattering in her yard.

But she had never seen it.

Now, of course, she was too old to believe it. She knew the power and destruction of the heavenly fiery explosions. At just the right distance they nurture life. But too close, they consume; too distant, they freeze. Blinding fire, brittle ice. And somewhere between the thin sliver of life.   (Unpublished manuscript)

While driving a stretch of highway one afternoon, the visual and tactile sensations of the Big Dipper's stars falling to earth suddenly filled my thought. It was not a jolt, just a gentle, complete awareness. I don't know what triggered the vision. That afternoon I wrote the first three paragraphs quoted.

Sometime later, when Morgan's character and problems were becoming more apparent, I wrote the last paragraph. By then, I was consciously looking for a contrast to the falling stars—a seasoned, more cynical perspective on the stars—and I remembered that the sun was just the right distance away to nurture life on earth. The words "blinding fire, brittle ice" slapped me across the face. I knew the story was telling me something important here. I was listening.

The words "thin sliver of life" whooshed the entire story into a single stream. The great-grandfather and Morgan shared a problem: their lives were thin slivers, not rounded lives that spilled generously over the edges. Theirs had a nervous thinness, the feeling that there was not enough time or resources for them to find themselves. This niggardly tightness had pressed down layer upon layer on the great-grandfather's life; it was only a potential for Morgan. But Morgan could become a shadow of the great-grandfather, unless . . .

In the first instance, on the highway, a vision that seemed to come whole from nowhere, a gift, became a leading metaphor for the story. I had been listening intently for some time prior to this. What I gained was mostly a sense of the tone of the story. This sense was prophetic of the vision I had in the car of stars falling. I knew, when I felt it, that it was something for the book. My focus in the car had certainly not been on the book. But all my listening had saturated the back of my mind with the tone of the story. This saturated background served as an open, loose focus.

In the second instance, words triggered by that previous vision led me to the particular problem of the story's characters, an important theme of the story. I sensed immediately that these words matched the potential of the story that had been speaking to me from the beginning. Here, I focused tightly on the words to know their meaning.

What fascinated me about this—and this was typical of my process—was that the result seemed wonderfully creative by my standards; yet I got there not by trying to be creative, but by trying very hard to *listen* deeply to what the gift metaphor and the words were saying to me about the story. The product was so right; *and its rightness included creativity.*

Earlier, when my focus was to be creative, no insightful, appropriate ideas jumped to mind. Why? Perhaps because writing stories (which need to grow organically) is not the same as the creative solving of discrete problems. Perhaps listening, an aspect of intuition, is a unique way of thinking that leads to creative solutions and must be taught differently than typical creativity techniques.

But such listening is learned only by experience and a commitment to truth—a willingness to follow the voice even if we distrust what it says.

Truth. It permeates my definition of creativity. When I write, I strain to hear the inner voice. I ask myself, Am I telling the truth? Is what I am saying firmly rooted either in the story or in my experience? Does it emanate from the still, deep waters? Or is it something that sounds clever, something I have heard before? So much of what we say and write emanates from the layer of busy, everyday chatter that separates us from our truest thoughts. The layer is dense; we must penetrate it in order to hear the rock-solid truths of our own experience and consciousness.

When we speak from what we truly know and feel, our words vibrate with truth that is directly *felt* by listeners and ourselves before we *understand* it. Its immediacy and power seem independent of, unburdened by, words. This vibration of truth activates intuitive communication. While science connects us to understanding by reasoned steps, art connects us to truth by intuition.

Originality does not mean being the first to say something that's never been said. It means saying exactly what *you* know. It means your expression matches the truth within you. So I find I must focus like a laser on honesty and precision. While I am writing, all my energy fixes on seeing honestly and bringing what I see into focus with words. If we are each an original, then originality is the accurate reflection of what we see and are.

But telling the truth is difficult if my focus is to create or invent. For instance, while writing this book, I felt the pressure to come up with something strikingly inventive. The temptation to make things up or to adapt what others had already articulated so well was often unconscious. But I found that if I begin with fabrication or adaptation, I do not work outward from the place where ideas germinate in my own thinking. I am off-center, out-of-balance. The words are lies—or at best, half-truths—because they are floating loose, unconnected to the deepest ground within. The writing does not work. Perhaps because lies have no coherence, no grounding, one cannot success-fully *tell* a lie. However, if I listen carefully to the still, quiet truth within and wait for the words to align with it and define it, there is coherence. Then the writing works.

Coherence characterizes the voice of the story. Michael Polanyi, distinguished professor of physical chemistry and philosopher, discusses coherence, or things pulling together, in the context of science. His comments apply as well to my writing process:

> . . . the scientist has hunches, and elated by these an-ticipations, pursues the quest that should fulfill these anticipations. This quest is guided throughout by feelings of a deepening coherence, and these feelings have a fair chance of proving right. We may recognize here the powers of a dynamic intuition. The mechanism of this power can be illuminated by an analogy. Physics speak of potential energy that is released when a weight slides down a slope. Our search for deeper coherence is guided by a potentiality. We feel the slope toward deeper insight as we feel the direction in which a heavy weight is pulled along a steep incline. It is this dynamic intuition which guides the pursuit of discovery.
>
> (In Vaughan, 150)

Seeking truth demands that we plumb the depths of our own consciousness. Yet truth is universal. Writing stories is listening deep to our own truth and discovering its universality. It is digging through our own backyard to reach China.

But I find truthful writing a challenge. Before the blinking cursor has finished sputtering three or four sentences, I know they are somehow "off." Not quite the truth. I send the cursor back to review the words, matching them against a vague sense of what I am really trying to say. More words, more cursor relays. Eventually, the words approximate the truth. But I am usually dissatisfied.

Because it is so hard to get at, truth demands attentive listening, stillness. It requires a tight, concentrated focus. It must close out the diverting surface chatter. Saul Bellow says,

> I feel that art has something to do with the achievement of stillness in the midst of chaos. A stillness which characterizes prayer, too, and the eye of the storm. I think that art has something to do with an arrest of attention in the midst of distraction.
>
> (In Winokur, 25)

"Entering in" helps me attain this still focus. Like an actor who becomes his role, a writer is a taut string vibrating with every true tone of the story. If she loosens her firm focus on the story, the writing wobbles off pitch. The story becomes something that is happening to her. But when the writer is outside the story (like the actor merely reciting his lines) the writing loses power. The focus is a tenuous one. We can lose it as easily as a motorist who suddenly finds he is looking at the bugs on the windshield instead of the view of the countryside sliding by.

A listening writer does not feel like a creator or director. Novelist Katherine Paterson tells about her children asking the question that bugs all high school students in required English classes: "'Mom, when a writer writes all that stuff down, they don't know what it means, do they? . . . We're supposed to find all these symbols and explain them. I bet the writers don't even know they're in there, right?'" (133–34).

Paterson's answer? "If they do, they're probably not very good writers."

If the writer is a creator-director trying to think of inventive plots and solutions, she has not entered into the story. She works somewhere outside it.

I learned that *what* I focused on was the voice of the story and truth; *how* I focused was with both a dispersed and a concentrated attention.

As I attended to the voice of the story and my listening, I began to notice wild fluctuations in focus. I saw myself consistently trying to do two things in different degrees: on the one hand, to restrict my thought and effort to a narrow, tight, energized focus; and on the other, to allow a loose, open, passive focus. Before I recognized this, I was happily ignorant; afterward, I felt hopelessly torn and tormented. Was this tension some kind of mental static trying to scramble my work? Was it some inscrutable requirement of productive creativity? Or was it simply a natural, friendly process?

At first, laser focus—entering in, listening—impressed me. I began to feel the only way I could be productive was to become a tight wad of concentrated focus. Listen, obey, listen, obey. Intense. Exhausting.

That exhaustion demanded I find a gentler focus. The needed relief came with my discovery of dispersed, or satellite, focus. And, once again, I learned it's not either/or. No part of writing is a clean satellite or laser focus. It's mixed. Like an automatic lens, focus constantly shifts from closed to open, active to passive, tight to loose, concentrated to diffused.

❧ ❧ ❧

HUNTERS AND DREAMERS

A deer hunter patrols the woods. He looks at nothing in particular, but remains fixed on the whole scene—all its movement, smells, sounds—so that he misses nothing. His focus is intense but diffused.

While writing stories, I am the hunter. Shadows of characters, plots, and themes fill my mental environment. I am alert, consciously or unconsciously, to every visitor to my woods.

Sometimes diffused focus is intense—watching like a hunter; sometimes it's more relaxed—watching like a dreamer. Writer Brenda Ueland describes it as a "passive clarity":

. . . I know that imagination comes, works, when you are *not* trying, when you have a peculiar passive clarity. A friend of mine has frequently the same dream. In it a procession of people begin coming, all strange and unknown, with fascinating faces and costumes, and she thinks in her dream when she sees them coming: "Oh, good! Here they come!" as though it were a parade for her own delectation. She makes no effort, just deliciously relaxes. And I think it is something like this that characters in your story or your novel come before you and show themselves. (160)

Dispersed focus is alertness without trying or forcing. It's like climbing around in a favorite tree. I follow its branches, avoiding the weak ones. (This subtle alertness is to keep from falling—from waking up.) I enjoy each view as the branches summon me upward, outward. When I come upon a particularly compelling view—or a really comfortable hollow to sit in—I rest there. I give my thoughts over to the view or the comfortable silence. But the view, the silence, doesn't just sit there. It takes my thoughts and leads them to new insights.

Loose attention is especially important in research. It allows connections among ideas that seem to *want* to meet, thoughts that naturally cohere but may not be combined by the rational mind.

When I was first drawn to the story about a carousel I saw it taking place on an island off the coast of Maine. However, I was feeling at the same time an odd predilection toward Scotland, particularly the Isle of Skye (which, honestly, seemed more related to my traveling instincts than the story). Meanwhile, historical research told me the story had to take place in France. I was jumping all over the globe.

But two incredible, serendipitous pieces of information leapt to my attention, not only tying these places together but giving a structure to the unfolding story. I was rummaging around in travel books, researching my trip to Scotland, and in French history sources, finding information for the story, when two historical events dropped separately into my lap.

Around the time of forerunners of the carousel in medieval France, a group of Scottish soldiers (conceivably from the Isle of Skye) joined Joan of Arc in the Battle of Orleans to some acclaim. Later, crofters on the Isle of Skye were ordered off the island and taken to resettle in what is now Nova Scotia (making the idea of those Scottish soldiers in France having ancestors on an obscure island off Maine's coast plausible). These facts thus neatly solved a puzzle I didn't even know I was working. They fit powerfully with my intuitive plans and were an obvious signal guiding me into the story.

If I had been digging for specific information or for some as yet unknown idea to solve a particular puzzle, would I have noticed these amazing facts? I am convinced I saw them because my dispersed focus was wide open, ready for anything. I felt that somehow the story was sifting through a beach full of sand grains to bring the right ones to my attention.

Such occurrences are typical of the many serendipitous events that impel all my writing. I have come to trust that they will appear. I am alert to their approach but have little control over their visits.

Many people would toss off such occurrences as coincidence, but some law seems to be operating here. Perhaps it underlies Thucydides' observation, "Stories happen to those who tell them" (in Calkins, 170). Perhaps the more we breathe life into our writing, the more our life draws breath back from the writing.

No matter how much research I do, no matter how long the work simmers on the back burner, the connection or insight always comes as a gift. It strikes with awe in the same way this evening's sunset will when I drive home along the river. It is as if I do not expect it. I suppose it is the same for the hunter. I think this is because my real work is to keep a diffused focus, to yield and wait rather than to make something happen. The hours of research and rational thinking are not the work that leads directly to the insight. They seem ancillary to the real "work" of keeping the focus passive. When I yield or wait for something, it is a gift, not a product of my effort.

At the 1990 Boston Globe–Horn Book Awards ceremony for outstanding children's-book authors, three of the six recipients remarked on serendipity. Paul Fleischman called serendipity "one of the four food groups." Jerry Spinelli said, "It happens when you're not looking. You have to make yourself passive—receptive. Something visits you." Ed Young felt it was important to be "alert—in a passive way."

I respond automatically to research by loosening, relaxing, playing. It is like knowing when to push during a birth, only the opposite, knowing when to pull back and relax. It is the same as deciding to write a novel but never admitting it to the deeper parts of yourself. It is looking to the side.

While open focus was necessary during the conceptual stages of the story, "looking to the side" was a helpful variation during the actual writing. Flutist Jean-Pierre Rampal is known for the almost human sounds of his tone. When asked how he achieved these sounds, he answered, "I perform best when I forget my flute is there. . . . You must never play the flute as though it were only a flute." In like manner, I decide to express something through words, but immediately I expand the focus. I must never write as if my medium were only words. I must write as a composer, a painter, a sculptor. The words have grain, color, rhythm and cadence, tone—the bright major key, the yearning minor. I must connect the medium—words—to other aspects of life. That means looking *around* and *to the side* of the writing. This allows thought to *expand* into expression rather than be confined by it. (So it allays my fear that words will limit or deform the inspired thought.)

When I look up at the stars from the field next to my summer cabin, one shines more brightly than the others. But as I focus on it, the brightness fades. If, instead, I focus on the black darkness near it, its brightness grows again in the corner of my eye. It is a frustrating tease. I cannot look directly at it. It will be bright only in the corner of my eye. I am not in control here.

During walks I notice that when I am excited by a new insight, I instinctively jump back. It is the hunter's instinct: don't get too close, maintain a wide field of vision, hold it in context before it flies. If I move in tight, it will skitter out of my grasp like a kitten outdoors. I have to keep my distance, sneak around it, and most important, fake an air of nonchalance. I am serious, but I have to play a little to keep it within my grasp.

Or maybe this pulling back is a neurotic fear of focusing, closing in. When we get too close we see things as they really are. They lose their mystique. And it is the mystique that inspires me in the first place. I do not want to lose it.

Or maybe it is *I* who am the hunted.

> Where does the idea for a novel come from? . . . The fruitful idea may well spring from something we see out of the corner of the eye. . . . It begins to *haunt*. . . . It is not so much that one chooses a subject, as that *it* chooses *one*. (Sarton, 26)

Uh-oh. Ideas pursue *me*. And I live in *their* woods. Jerry Spinelli says, "Ideas bite you like mosquitoes."

The more I have watched my thinking processes, the more I realize that I do not conjure up ideas deliberately or even voluntarily. An idea is something that happens to me more than something I do.

Lightning strikes. Daylight dawns. Fire.

Creative process is characterized by intuition, born of an open, receptive, anticipatory state of mind. Diffused focus is intuition's playground. It *allows* creation; it doesn't cause it. It expands our vision so we can see the connections that give impetus to the story or characters. It explains serendipity as the gift that always appears when we wait and yield—put our effort toward keeping an open focus. It shows us ideas out of the corner of the eye. It teaches us how ideas come: we do not manufacture them and we cannot chase them down. We must coax them. We must be receptive, ready, and alert for their appearing.

🍎 🍎 🍎

BALANCING FOCUSES

In the toy-box on my desk I have a small spinning top shaped like a mushroom. After a good long spin on its cap, it wobbles and then takes a surprise flip to stand on its slender stem. It's a delight every time. (That's why I never gave it to my four-year-old friend for whom it was intended.)

A similar wobble-and-flip often occurs when I'm in a productive passive focus. I may be at my desk or in bed, dreaming or fantasizing a procession of inspired ideas. I feel invigorated, yet relaxed. Pretty soon the physical relaxation overtakes the mental vigor. Wobble. This is the dangerous stage. One of two things happens: I naturally switch to an active, laser focus and begin a productive writing spell . . . Flip. Or I dally in dangerous diversions just a little too long . . . Z-z-z-z-z.

When I realized how helpful passive focus was for receiving appropriate ideas, I was tempted into a constant state of dreaming, musing, looking to the side or out of the corner of my eye—being available. I allowed myself to be stimulated by my environment to the point of exhaustion. Every exterior or interior image that came along seemed to carry some sort of potential relevance. People's conversations, the sounds of nature, passing thoughts. I was *too* open. But I was also green enough to feel guilty about narrowing my focus and shrinking the depth of field.

During a walk that had allowed ample open focus, I felt impelled to finish a story. I saw that I needed an utterly closed, laser focus to do it. When I returned to the house, I went with clear, determined direction to the office, switched on the computer, and wrote myself out of the open focus and into a closed one. This invigorated me and brought a satisfying sense of accomplishment. I'm sure it had happened many times before, but it felt particularly good because I knew for the first time the pleasant balance between closed and open focus.

At other times I needed to be sure a tight focus did

not interrupt or dominate my dreaming, my openness. As in meditation and prayer, it's often a discipline to stay passively and openly focused. There are specific times for satellite and for laser focus. I must listen to the voice of the story and the voice of my life, to know which one, when.

Having said that, a truer statement might be that passive and active focus (or open and closed focus) are going on together much of the time. While I was writing a short story about ice fishing I was aware that my concentration was riveted to the walk out over the ice to the fishing hole. Yet I sensed my passive focus on another part of the story having to do with the tone of a conversation taking place near the climax (which I didn't know yet). I was aware of this tone and a developing dialogue. It was working its way like a worm loosening the underground. But I was also certain that I shouldn't focus on it directly. I needed to leave it underground until it—and the writer—were ready. It was amazing to watch that happening, but it was only a fleeting moment of observation, something to be seen—again—out of the corner of my eye. That interval of passive focus required no discipline for it to continue other than the discipline to leave it alone, to look away from it.

FLOW

When dispersed and concentrated attention dance as one, creative work finds a flow. Whole concentration. Absolute attention. When I lose consciousness of a self separate from the work, I am alive to the whole—the core of ideas held in concentrated focus and a gathering fringe of ideas in loose focus. This heightened attention includes whole and part, inside and outside, as one. When I am one with this flow, I feel the work fulfill the promises of inspiration—potential, discovery, adventure, covered ground, progression, purposeful motion—and of coherence— things falling together and working together.

In his book entitled *Flow,* Mihaly Csikszentmihalyi characterizes this state as providing "a creative feeling of transporting the person into a new reality" (74). This "new reality" is the essence of creation. It is at once the call and the prize of creative endeavor.

Painter Robert Henri describes the power a sense of flow has over the artist:

> The object, which is back of every true work of art, is the attainment of a state of being, a state of high functioning, a more than ordinary moment of existence. In such moments activity is inevitable, and whether this activity is with brush, pen, chisel, or tongue, its result is but a by-product of the state, a trace, the footprint of the state. These results, however crude, become dear to the artist who made them because they are records of the state of being which he has enjoyed and which he would regain.   (159)

The hunger for this "high functioning" drives me to write.

But finding this flow is usually an ordeal. It's a tug-of-war between frustration over vague inspiration that cannot find its form and the strong intuition that affirms there *is* form. This sputtering, stopping and starting over, nearly exhausts me. I know I will have to run (probably crawl) over mountains of discouragement and through valleys of boredom and lost meaning. I know what lies ahead: troubling, big time.

Getting through this preflow stage depends on the power of intuition—the range of the voice—and on listening. Listening, and obediently following, leads to dispersed and concentrated attention. (This is a law.) The listening feels like intense play. It is yielding; losing myself and giving in to the work. And that yielding takes effort and concentration, because my normal mode of operation is either to control or to avoid the work altogether.

Of course, there are levels of flow. But feelings of being carried, riding a wave, mark all of them.

Sometimes flow feels like homing:

> When I write, I feel it all on the tip of my tongue. The words seek to align with this forgotten thing, this goal. There is a feeling of flow because my eye is on this goal—however vague—and I can feel the words merging with it as they define it. (Process notes)

Sometimes a simple sense of rightness carries me forward without a goal:

Today I wrote a dialogue between Morgan and her father. I had no idea what to do; no epiphany, no tone guided me. I believed that a conversation between Morgan and her father would divulge something about them and, maybe, about the plot that had recently gone flat. At the beginning the line of words was pushing through mud. But then, it was like some force plucked the writing out of my hands. The dialogue flowed until I reached an exchange that I didn't understand, but seemed to carry important meaning. It was teasing me, telling me something new about Morgan and the story.   (Process notes)

That was another kind of flow. It mixed the adrenalin of hitting a rich vein with the anxiety of not knowing where the vein would lead. So much potential! I did not know exactly what the dialogue meant when I wrote it, but I did not want to pin it down, ask it a lot of questions, either. I just wanted to keep writing and trust that sometime something would be said, something would happen, that would illuminate what was hidden.

The appetite for discovery fuels flow. And discovery is distinct from creating. I feel that story characters are *real.* My delight is in unfolding, discovering their lives and stories, not in creating them. It is the difference between entering into and living the story and looking into and directing the story from without.

Flow carries in it no sense of creating. I cannot remember ever having *decided* to make a poem or write a story. Essays, poems, stories, always come to me. I don't go out searching for them. I simply stand available to their approach . . . waiting, watching.

Flow and Technique

Flow is the optimal state for both the artist and the audience, because it allows meaning. This awakening of meaning is communication. And writing, like all art, is communication—primarily between the artist and the voice of the work and secondarily between the artist and audience.

While writing or thinking about current work, my focus cannot be on creativity or the desire to do something original. More specifically, I cannot center on *techniques* of creativity or writing. I must put all my concentration and effort into listening to the voice of the story (through dispersed and concentrated attention), letting intuition guide, letting go, losing myself. Everything else—techniques, creativity heuristics, writing rules, story schemata—is certainly required but must be subsidiary for me to do the best work.

Michael Polanyi has written much about focus. Here, he illustrates two types:

> My correspondence arrives at my breakfast table in various languages, but my son understands only English. Having just finished reading a letter I may wish to pass it on to him, but must check myself and look again to see in what language it was written. I am

vividly aware of the meaning conveyed by the letter, yet know nothing whatever of its words. I have attended to them closely but only for what they mean and not for what they are as objects. If my understanding of the text were halting, or its expressions or its spelling were faulty, its words would arrest my attention. They would become slightly opaque and prevent my thought from passing through them unhindered to the things they signify. (5)

Polanyi is speaking about flow. The reader (and I will add, the writer) has a focal (primary) awareness of meaning and a subsidiary (secondary) awareness of words. If as a writer I focus primarily on tools and techniques, the flow of what I am expressing will be lost. Similarly, if the reader falls (or is led) into analyzing my words for their technique, literary value, and style, he is focusing on something other than meaning and experience. The flow will be interrupted, and meaning will become opaque.

Like Polanyi's fluid skill at foreign languages, the writer's or artist's technique must be developed enough to allow her and her readers or viewers to focus primarily on the heart of the work—to listen to its voice and find meaning.

Does this mean that a writer must *master* technique before writing something meaningful? No. We must continually gather the straight lines of cause and effect into the circles of both/and. Otherwise, chicken-and-egg problems will frustrate all our work. New techniques, new tools, grow within a state of creative flow. When focus functions at such a high level, it gathers surrounding elements in ways that will be useful for the work's purpose. In this process, the writer happens upon new modes of thought of which she may be largely unaware. Even a little technique, a little writing fluidity, when accompanied by inspiration and a listening humility, can open the gates. Poetry issues from within. When its current is strong enough to carry away obstructions, even the lack of technique cannot stop it.

❦ FOUR ❦

Earth

The ocean floor rises into mountains that float as islands on the sea. Land under water and land above water are one earth.

But we know the dry land in a way we cannot know the underwater earth. We trust the earth surrounded by light and air in a way we cannot trust the earth shrouded in fluid darkness. Our inclination is to avoid the deep.

In the ocean shallows, a toddler dangles at the end of his mother's outstretched arms. As the waves cast the giggling child out toward sea and suck him back, he is grounded by his mother's firm stand on the earth under water. In time, the child will learn that the water itself supports him. He will wriggle free of his mother's fingers and swim, delighting in the freedom and gasping at the power of the waves.

Like the child, the writer plays on the surface of the deep. In the necessary chaos and tension of creation she bobs and lurches. Without firm ground beneath, she must learn to swim in the chaos, to release herself to creation's experience. The first lessons for child and writer are in letting go and trusting the natural forces that support the body and impel the creative work.

Sometime after these first lessons, a deeper awareness pulls at the writer. Beyond the pleasure of riding waves, the elementary accomplishments of sculling, diving, and rolling, lies the mastery of forces that turns power to her advantage. But in order to pursue this mastery, the writer needs a strengthening vision. She needs to reach far enough down into the deep to touch the earth beneath.

This hidden earth was for me the essence of the writing experience, the motivation for my creative processes. Desire to know this ground, *walk* it, squish it between my toes, rose stronger than the urge to write. In order to continue writing, I had to know the earth that supported and nourished me as a writer.

It is obvious to me now that we each need a personal vision of the underwater earth that grounds our writing or art. This unfolding vision is the spine of our work. If we are totally unconscious of it, we write without its buttressing lift. Then the body of our work is unaligned, drooping like a marionette with no one to manipulate its invisible but life-giving strings.

Nonetheless, we bring the underwater earth nearer the surface of consciousness not so much for the work's sake as for our own. For the artist finds her life not in the things she creates but in the *experience of creation*. And the fullness of that experience depends largely on the artist's awareness of the universe behind her work—finding her particular mission, her particular joy and strength in writing. But this is necessarily a personal vision. I can tell you what I have noticed of my earth. It may resonate with some previously unheard overtones in your own writing experience. Or it may annoy, even anger you. At the very least, any response to another writer's experience—affirmative or contrary—will call forth aspects of your own.

Early in the research on my own creative processes, what had previously seemed unapproachable mysteries emerged as much mystical as mysterious. In other words, while hidden from the rational mind, these undeclared mysteries can be approached by other ways of knowing, ways that allow mystery to expand alongside knowing, ways that relish the wonder at the incomprehensible.

In a long-lost book about flying insects, I read an interesting interpretation of magic that I think applies to mystery as well. The author argued that magic is knowledge known only by a few. He predicted that as knowledge expands, relatively fewer and fewer people will be privy to the same knowledge. This has already happened. We see it in medical and consumer information. Although the knowledge is "out there," we lack the time and wherewithal to get to it. Information-processing technology keeps promising us that we *will* have the capability. But information continues to explode faster than the technology to manage it, and we feel individually that we know less and less what we need to know. As science pumps more and more information into the life stream, mystery seems to be gaining rather than diminishing. In an odd turn, science may be serving mystery as much as knowledge.

However, intuition has always recognized its partnership with mystery. It accepts that while we may "know" something, we will never comprehend it, grasp it completely. Intuition thereby fosters a certain humility in knowing. I recognized that the earth beneath my writing calls me to know it on its own terms. I must not analyze it but entertain it. I must come into its presence simply to notice what it offers of itself. I must attend to it.

With a naive faith, I stepped into the deep. Handing intuition its due credentials, I gave it authority. I began to trust my felt experience more than the "reality" of writing I had been taught. No longer satisfied with a subconscious awareness, I yearned to know more of the core and expanse of this felt experience. New touchstones surfaced—probably ancient and universal, but new and personal to me.

❧ ❧ ❧

THE THREE I'S

When I think of creativity, it falls naturally into a setting of inspiration, intuition, and insight. They are hopelessly intertwined, but I can differentiate them somewhat.

Inspiration tingles my consciousness with an awareness that I am in the company of something special. This "something" harbors a potential that sometimes bursts forth, sometimes unfolds like petals. The "pleasurable nag" beckons me toward writing with its promise of surprise insights and cathartic climaxes. It tantalizes with the belief that, this time, troubling will not interrupt the glorious path. Then, once again, I learn that troubling *is* the path. Inspiration is intuitive in its power and vagueness. It is never rational.

At the impulse of inspiration, intuition enjoins reason and knowledge of writing schemata and leads thought toward insight—the sudden and comprehensive flash of understanding that relaxes into relief. Chaos shifts into cosmos. Intuition, the large name for ways of knowing distinct from reason, alternately slides and gropes toward some veiled thing in the distance (or into total darkness, for that matter). This nonrational cognition guides the entire process of creation by sensing something round and whole—something needing clarifying rather than development through reason. Hope, not doubt, saturates intuition. Intuition and insight inspire me, fill me with energy, move me.

The three i's can appear after periods of hard work or "out of the blue." Together, they form the ground from which my work emanates, where seeds grow into full-blown expression. If I am separated from this ground, I do not write.

I discovered inspiration, intuition, and insight working within the spirit of potential and the tensions of opposite ways of being, knowing, and working. I recognized their smooth cycle and interaction. I saw how dispersed and concentrated attention brought them forth. But the source of the three i's lies in deeper ground.

❦ ❦ ❦

WORDLESSNESS AND THE WORD

Our world overflows with words: spoken words, printed words, words running through our minds, media words and next-door words, people talking at one another, people talking to themselves. In this blizzard of words, listening is tough. Even in silence, I sometimes think I hear chatter leaking from the airwaves surrounding the telephone, radio, and TV. Can there be such a thing as silence? Everybody's talking. Nobody's listening. In their plea for our attention, words are suffocating us.

And yet, if I am honest, I know that a true listener not only can redeem some of the words (just as a truly imaginative reader can redeem vacant writing) but is able to hear the silence above the din. Possibly at least part of the answer to the cacophony is to hear better rather than shut it out.

I have thought often of a saying attributed to Martin Buber: "You should utter words as though heaven were opened within them and as though you did not put the word into your mouth, but as though you had entered the word." Perhaps a legitimate adaptation might be: We should *hear* words as though heaven were opened within them and as though someone did not put the words in our ear, but as though we had entered the word.

Trapped in a boring conversation, we try to listen with some interest. My brother-in-law, a professor, often comments on the ability of good students to find personal connections to boring lectures (not his!) and maintain their concentration. When we give something our attention, it tends to take on importance and interest. But there are deeper lessons to listening. I remember one such lesson from years ago.

As I sat in a church listening to a minister read from the Bible, my eyelids were engaged in the weight-lifting contest of their lives. If they dropped, my neck would surely weaken next, and soon my head would be bobbing in rapturous sleep. It was a small congregation, and I was a visitor who wanted to be polite. I put every brain cell on guard and listened. What happened in my own thoughts kept me awake. I noticed that as I listened, many other thoughts, quite off the subject, darted into consciousness—all kinds of thoughts, some of them particularly productive and needed. I felt refreshed, not drained, when I left the church.

I didn't think about this event afterward. But one day years later, it came abruptly to mind, and I realized that there was some relationship between focused listening and receptivity to ideas. I realized how often it happened that when I tried to listen to empty words, when I gave up a little of my why-should-I-be-subjected-to-this ego, many fresh, productive ideas came to the fore.

It is the opposite of what I supposed. I unconsciously thought that in order to listen for new ideas, one should be surrounded by silence. But that is not the case. What is required is focused listening, a receptivity somehow as open to oblique ideas as to those directly related.

And the same is true with writing. By entering into the word—into the realm where something valuable is speaking to us—we hear. No, the words with our neighbor over the fence are, typically, not inspired nuggets of wisdom and insight. But—and *I* surely can't explain this—somehow our listening as if the words were important causes us to hear not only our neighbor's words, but other, silent words that have nothing to do with our neighbor. When we're listening, the ideas are biting.

But that's the ideal. Some days, I still want to smash the TV or yank out the tinny car radios blaring at every stoplight.

Having made the case for words, there is, predictably, another side to the coin. I know that I need wordlessness. I find it in wind and water, all nature; in music, art, and dance; in babbling babies; in rhythms. Writers need inspired relief from words.

And I know I need silence too. Within and without. No words, no wordless sound.

Traditionally, we attach notions of intuition and insight to wise men, mystics, poets, saints—people who radiate an inner stillness. Before I knew much about how writers live and work, I included them in the group. But most writers are not poets. A writer's mind is filled with the clamor of words and information and the constant strain of trying to shunt ideas onto a track of words. It's not a quiet place. Writers are not necessarily contemplative, though they spend much of their time thinking. Like war reporters literally in the heat of battle, many writers do their best work with a churning stomach and mortars blasting around them. An overcharged life brings out the best concentration. While most writers demand some degree of outer silence, their desire, need, for inner silence fluctuates widely.

But in order to tune consciousness to elusive frequencies, we need inner as well as outer silence. I think it has to do with how much a writer leans on intuition. If we write solely on the level of problem solving and "what next?" curiosity, employing games of reason and cause and effect, the work may draw little from the deep. But the very nature of poetry and some types of narrative calls for long drafts from deeper wells.

The word "contemplation" brings one to the word "center." People talk about "finding their center," "becoming centered." But my life and work are centered on words, talk, errands, responsibilities, the telephone, computer, and car. I am not centered on silence. I have to chip off pieces of silence and wordlessness from dense days. I find wordlessness and silence on the edges of life, not at its center of home and work. And where wordlessness and silence are found, writing abounds. I write and create on the edges, at the borders of life, not at the center.

BORDERLANDS

A hike along the bluffs of the Mississippi offers more than a view of the great river carving the boundary between Illinois and Missouri. Where the highlands meet the valley, two robust ecosystems overlap. This fertile borderland is rich in plants, birds and animals, geologic specimens, and history. A similar fertility thrives at the borders where two or more ideas meet. I spoke earlier about this, the generative power of connecting ideas in creative tension, the tension of paradox.

But "borderland" can also mean the antithesis of fecundity; it often signifies a lonely outpost and carries with it an end-of-the-world connotation. The thick web of a dynamic civilization wears thin as it disperses into the hinterlands. Not much happens where the waning edge of one civilization meets the waxing edge of another. Borders are nonproductive.

Before I looked carefully into my own creative processes, I had little respect for the borders within my days. I either ignored them in sustained morning-to-night activity or accepted them as wasteland.

We wake up to an alarm or to equally alarming music and jump into the day at full speed, never appreciating the dreaming edge of sleep—the border between sleeping and waking. Or when the rim of night appears on the horizon, our bodies and minds may sense the changing light and the wistful air, but we douse such perceptions with a flood of television.

A day bloated with busyness and words has no grace. It either burdens us or falsely satisfies us with the belief that the more we do and say, the more life we have. This "life" has erased the day's seasons—no more dawn, morning, noon, evening, sunset, and all the borders in between. There is only full-orbed "day."

We deny ourselves the fertility of the borders within daily life. We cut out the natural buffers between activities and nature's cycles for the sake of efficiency and responsibility. Or we miss the productivity of borders because we think of them as fallow fields.

While I was writing this book, fringe areas began to emerge in bas-relief. Gradually, I became aware of the times before sleep and prior to waking as distinct seasons holding their own rhythms not to be ignored.

Every night I sat in bed in the darkness and watched the shape of the windows and the shadows of trees appear. The dark and quiet usually brought relief and gratitude. The day's words and events rested quietly on the edges of thought. I felt disturbances recede. I didn't think in the day's purposeful way, but I was alert and resisted sleep for the pleasure of stillness. I let thoughts rise and fall. Meditation, communion, prayer, materialized from the soft yearning about whatever came to mind. Mostly I listened.

In the morning, on the other side of sleep, I did not

jump out of bed. Up until then, guilt usually catapulted me into a standing position of sorts. But I began to shed the guilt of staying in bed, because I noticed what good, clear, and truthful thoughts were surfacing before I actually wakened to the day and its demands. I rarely gain insight from dreams, but the period of waking often seems more lucid than what some would call full consciousness. In this borderland, ideas loosen from their moorings and float around, associating with other thoughts. Insights, free from the constraints of the business of daily life, abound.

As I allowed the border between sleep and full waking to stretch, I was amazed at and satisfied with its productivity. Perhaps it is during waking rather than in awakened consciousness that we are most alert and receptive. In this period undirected by me, answers to troubling home or work situations often slipped in. Writing snags were solved at deeper and more satisfying levels than the solutions found by day. It was pure pleasure because it was a gift. I was an alert and grateful listener; it did not seem effortful. But this period has its natural duration. Always there comes the moment for full waking, the moment when I recognize the border time has fulfilled its part.

Although I can usually sit up as late as I want and take advantage of the time before sleep, life rarely allows the border of waking its due. But I try now to give at least a few minutes to softening and expanding waking's hard edge. Finally, I've given credit to these borderlands for shouldering much of my work. They certainly contribute ideas and insights, but I think their most important work is toning and shaping thought generally—harmonizing opposing attitudes and ideas, softening the extremes, clarifying the muddled, lending grace.

Once I became aware of the borders between sleep and waking, other edges began to bulge and stretch. When I could distinguish the tempers of morning and evening from the rest of the day, certain kinds of activity and work made sense at certain times.

Most writing manuals and many writers advise us to write in the morning when we are fresh and undistracted. But try as I have, morning is not my writing time. My thought is rambunctious then, and there are too many "must-dos" screaming for my attention. I've discovered the best solution for me is to deal with the "musts" and then take my thoughts out for a walk in the fresh air. Walking calms and gives priority to thoughts.

After the walk, I do some "nonwriting." Some people call it free-writing, but it's important for me to take *all* pressure and expectation out of the process. So, I don't allow myself to think of it as writing at all. It's simply following thoughts around, watching them interact, playing with ideas for projects, and using a computer or pencil to do it.

The morning work feeds the afternoon work. Sometime during the afternoon I sideslip onto a writing track. This is "real" writing time, the work part. Now I *tell* myself I'm writing, and I bring to bear all the discipline and trickery needed to keep me at the desk. Depending on the writing task, sometimes I play "beat-the-clock"; other times I try to lose myself—and time—in the writing work.

I save some of the revising and editing work for the beginning of the next afternoon, because it's easy to get into revisions. It takes no discipline or cajoling. Once I'm revising, it's not a huge leap to the real writing.

Of course, this is only partly true. Life is not consistent enough for me to keep a disciplined schedule for long. This simply describes how the pieces fall for me right now. Often I cannot do the morning "nonwriting." Gee, often I can't do the afternoon writing either.

But the lesson has been learned. Now I watch for and respect the seasons of the day. And I guard their borders. When it is time to quit one activity and move to the next, I'm forced into a trapeze act. I am swinging back and forth in a comfortable rhythm when I know I have to release the bar. Then comes that uncertain, suspended moment. Will I connect with the next bar or will I fall into the air of nothing?

I change direction hesitantly. I shift gears slowly. Everything can be lost in the single suspended moment between what I'm doing now and what I'm supposed to do next. It's true in life. It's true in writing.

I try never to leave the desk unless I am in the absolute middle of something. If I take a break after finishing revisions, I'll probably never return to the desk to begin more creative work. But if I begin the new work immediately and break later after finding a rhythm and comfort level, I can be optimistic about the chances for returning.

The only work I count on is in the day's cracks and edges. I know, in these tiny, finite bits, I will perpetually *prepare* to write. While I'm walking, driving, cooking—whenever I am alone, and often when I'm not—I am writing in my mind. I suppose this is what all writers do. It includes word searches, finding metaphors and analogies, seeing into other people's lives, observing nature closely, listening in on others' conversations. It requires looking to the side of life, seeing beneath its surfaces, living consciously and alertly, noticing, and most of all letting intuition guide me. And I think this preparation, this writing—not at the center but in the borders, cracks, edges—is the fount of my nonwriting and my real writing.

❦ ❦ ❦

TIME AND NEVERTIME

When I quit my day job and took to writing full-time, I figured, Great! I'll just write nine to one every day and then I'll be able to finish all the other details of life in the extra time. Time was time. Writing time. Errand time. Kid time. Husband time. Time for church and schools. Time for cooking and cleaning. So I would put time for family and time for writing first. Everything else would fit in around the edges. "As long as I am disciplined," I announced, "it will work." Double whoops. How could I have known there are two kinds of time? And the two don't get along. They get in each other's way. They elbow each other, and neither gives way easily.

Time is the finite box into which we must squeeze all the activities of a mortal life: to-do lists, career and personal accomplishments, cleaning and maintaining, volunteer work, recreation, eating, sleeping, changing diapers, mowing the lawn, changing the oil, shopping. And there is never enough of it.

Unlike the child, the adult has lost touch with nevertime. Instead of enslaving, nevertime liberates. It is ample. It flows forward and backward. It stands still. It enfolds past and future. It is full focus and concentration—an absolute attention that allows dreaming, entering in, losing oneself in the minutiae and the immensities of the universe. The largeness of nevertime magnifies the smallest moments to enrich our lives even as they unfurl behind us into the past. And it is the secret of child and artist.

Time and nevertime do not overlap. A wall separates them. You can leap this wall anytime, but you cannot straddle it. It's one side or the other. Nevertime is my creative time. It is impossible for me to be in time, with all its distractions and demands, and think, listen, and write coherently. When I say I need to find time to write, I really mean I need to find nevertime.

Today, escape seems the only real reason to write. The time at the computer has flowed. No, that's not true.

What happened between consciousness and fingers was so thickly and perfectly woven, so completely engrossing, there was no time.

Then I glance at the clock. What?! I've been here for *three* hours! I forgot my dental appointment! Again? I missed the afternoon mail, the telephone appointment with Japh's math teacher and who knows what else. (Journal)

However pleasant nevertime may be, the sudden vault into time gives me a case of the bends. The shift to time means pressure—the same as if I had taken a few days vacation while all the bills, mail, and usual details of life did not. I return to a mountain of time trash.

The view from time is not the same. I look back on my nevertime with a discouraged eye. Only two pages in three hours? What a waste of time! How will you explain this meager achievement to your family or, worse, your editor? Just *what* were you *doing* all that time? What have you got to show for three hours?

And yet, the real pressure of writing or any creative endeavor is not that it takes large blocks and countless snitches of time, but that it requires stepping *out of* time *into* the receptive, intuitive, attentive focus of nevertime. It is not so much the depletion of time that is worrisome, but the leaving of it.

It's not easy to leap the wall. We need the desire and the skill to leap. Everything is so busy in time; it seems to affirm life. Only when the quantity of time oppresses us—too little for the adult, too much for the child—do we wish to escape it. In their lightness of being, children leap the wall all the time. Adults are sandbagged with responsibilities and guilt. Even if they desire nevertime, the gravity of life won't release them peaceably. Or maybe they have forgotten how to leap.

Nevertime feels good—productive, purposeful. It is the unpressured, receptive state of mind that breeds creative expression. But time will always tell you that, in fact, nevertime is a dawdler. Time's job is to deflate nevertime. Sure, without nevertime, there would be no creation. But slipping out of time never seems valid somehow. I learned that just as I need to embrace the waking border of sleep, so I must nurture nevertime, even if family and friends misunderstand or disapprove.

Once upon a Nevertime

It was just after dusk on Church Street Marketplace. Under the pale street lamps the dim rhythm of outdoor cafes and evening shoppers yielded to an odd stillness. In a scattered circle, adults and children stood transfixed as the faint, accordionlike whine of an English concertina drifted among them like smoke from a peace pipe. In the center I noticed a heavyset, long-haired and bearded man balanced on a rickety folding chair. He pumped the little black box with blacksmith's arms and squeezed Irish airs into the blue night. Next to him sat a table holding cassette tapes on sale for ten dollars. Only the music counted time. Time's rigid line slackened and curled around us in the Irish air. Past and future joined in nevertime. In a conscious dream, I could see myself folding a ten-dollar bill twice as I walked toward the musician. I could hear the tiny lapse in the music when he reached to take the bill as he had others. Then I felt his surprised hesitation when he realized I was placing it in his pocket. The music was broken and he smiled at my familiarity.

At that moment nevertime ceased. I was back in time. I took the ten-dollar bill from my wallet and folded it. Then every particular of the small exchange happened just as I had foreseen it. (Journal)

This event struck me, first, by the nevertime that waited for me to join it and, second, by the prophetic sense—a kind of second sight—that heightened the meaningfulness and importance of the experience.

Sometimes it seems that we see through time as a veil, not an impenetrable wall between what is and what might be. I am trying not to be weird here. I am not talking about paranormal experience. I am saying only that time is not the linear thing I thought it was and that there are everyday circumstances to prove it. This occurrence in the marketplace was one of those circumstances for me. I foresaw a tiny event. It happened as I saw it. It was not supernatural; it was *fundamentally* natural. These things happen every day in daydreams, déjà vu, incipient intuitions borne out in experience, momentary insights, sudden clarities.

I feel I should attend to these intuitions and then let them rest—refrain from drilling them with questions and badgering them for proof. I see through the glass darkly, never comprehending all. But understanding of this sort ripens through grace. I cannot impatiently and arrogantly rip off the veils. They will be shed naturally in growth. We grow in grace; we grow in our understanding of these things.

During such quiet out-of-time experiences the vagaries of creation are coalescing and shaping themselves into foundations for creative expression.

Nevertime can occur anywhere, anytime, unexpectedly or by invitation. This timeless sensation may occur as naturally at the desk as anywhere, but most often it has to be summoned through discipline, work-to-the-point-of-relaxation (as Ray Bradbury says), entering into the story, or fooling myself by "nonwriting" or "writing about."

The only problem is that as soon as I recognize I'm in nevertime, I've jumped out of it. (The reverse never happens when I realize I'm in time, though.) It has to do with watching myself, splitting myself in two: the observer and the actor being observed. The observer cannot enter nevertime. To gain entrance, she must be one with the actor. Does this mean that we shall never know the mysteries of nevertime, of flow, of the deep? Maybe.

SYNCHRONY AND SERENDIPITY

One of the aspects of nevertime is synchrony, which comes by way of Latin from the Greek meaning "same time." The writer lives in synchronies, and synchronies require nevertime.

When I wrote about the main character in my novel, I *was* my sixteen-year-old self. I was not trying to remember who I was back then. I still include that person. This is a simple truth about all of us. None of us is what we appear.

I made a surprise visit to Edith today. Her little yellow housebox sits off the slushy road right up against the hundred-foot white pines. Twenty years ago she left the Cape after her sister died and moved up here into the mobile home. She was sixty-five then. Most of her antique furniture would not fit, so she sold it or gave it to distant relatives. Now she lives off income from periodic auctions of her paintings and chairs at Sotheby's. Quarterly royalty checks for the musical arrangements she wrote during her piano career don't amount to much.

When I drove up the driveway today, she did not hear me as she usually does. As I walked up the skinny path dodging melting snowpiles, I heard Beethoven's C major piano concerto blaring right through the insulated walls and tightly shut doors. Then, in the picture window framed by icicles, I saw Edith. She stood in her plaid skirt and red cabled sweater with her back to me. Her arms flailed, pointing here at an imaginary string section, and her head bobbed, nodding now and then toward what must have been Paderewski at the piano. In her right hand she held a long pencil that came into focus only during the slow passages. I watched until the big finish when she collapsed in the silence onto her worn couch. A slight smile stretched her lips.

I waited a respectable time for her to catch her breath and then knocked on her door. (Journal)

Edith was in the synchrony of nevertime, where pasts, presents, and futures intertwine, where time is not a one-directional line but a multidimensional web. Like many old people, she had the gift of time travel, of breaking ranks from marching time. She was not merely an old lady. Her present self included all her past selves. When she showed me pictures of her seven-year-old self, I marveled at the impish eyes that continue to shine through the years. When she talked of Billy Diamond, her family's stableman who whistled her to sleep from the barn every night without ever knowing what it meant to her, she was the same young farmgirl. When she related the tragedy of her first marriage, she was the naive and vulnerable young wife. At any moment she was all the people she had ever been. Time had a way of curling around her rather than shooting straight forward. This explained to me why my own grandmother was sometimes embarrassingly co-quettish in her eighties. I would not be embarrassed now.

Encountering the fluidity of time in Edith's life awak-ened me to the fluidity of my own time. When I write I am all the selves I have ever been. Singly, by pairs, or in groups, they play into the writing. Larry Dossey says in his book *Space, Time & Medicine* that the Hopi Indians, like many primitive peoples, have no words for linear time. "They live in a kind of continual present that con-tains everything that has ever happened" (24).

A major motivation for doing any kind of art is the pleasure, the serenity, of time stopped. Nevertime gathers up the line of time into the eternal now. It relieves the pressures, the limitations, the finitude of time. Most of our silly attempts to thwart mortality are helpless in the face of time. Not plastic surgery, not bodybuilding, not health theories, not endless self-improvement, not more children, not money to buy new things—none of these can stop time, because they are *of* time. But stepping out of time into nevertime gives us a sense of infinity, im-mortality, truth. Nevertime links us to something we know is somehow true and right. It is another way of perceiving life apart from the accepted everyday view of time as linear. Nevertime allows the synchrony, the simul-taneity, of all things that the human mind spreads out along a line. Both modern physics and the ontology of primitive peoples align with nevertime. Through creative endeavor (true recreation, re-creation), meditation, prayer—through losing self—we escape time and its self-in-a-box.

When I was researching fireflies for the first story in the Midnight Naturalist series, I came upon this wondrous fact: During the summer somewhere in southeast Asia, Thailand I think, fireflies gather in the trees along the river. They come with their multitude of flashing rhythms, each a particular code for the appropriate mate. And when the trees are full of flashing lights an extraordinary event occurs. Suddenly they join together to send out a pulsating light in perfect synchrony. One who has seen it could not breathe for the beauty and power of the dark that vibrated with light. (I have never read of such a happening here, with North American fireflies.)

What could cause such a scene? What is behind any of the innumerable instances of sudden harmony and synchrony in chaotic nature? Chaos theorist Ilya Prigogine maintains that as a structure falls apart, some of its components will cooperate to bring about a transformation, a restructuring of the whole. He implies that somehow molecules "know" what they need to do to engender the renewal of the parent organism. Is this theory transferable to creativity in general? Do ideas associate intelligently in a way that will serve the as-yet-undiscovered story? Whether or not it is provable fact, this is certainly what I *feel* when I am writing a story.

Serendipity is defined as "the faculty for making fortunate and unexpected discoveries by accident." I love the paradox! So "chance" has skill behind it? And "chaos" is really the coming of new order? Next to the wonder of insight, serendipity is the single greatest motivation in my writing.

I had been listening to Bizet's opera *The Pearl Fishers* for a couple of weeks when I began to write one of the Midnight Naturalist stories that concerned ice fishing. While one particular duet played continually in the background, I studied smelts—abundant, six-inch, silver-and-green fish that come upriver with the tide. I wrote for a few days before the complete story idea with its related parts suddenly hit me. The story was about trying to attain the unattainable. Smelt fishing was easy and abundant—very unlike pearl fishing, where fishers can dive again and again without surfacing with a pearl. The smelt-fishing narrative needed the pearl-fishing metaphor to be a story. I felt the music had been telling me this all the while.

This amazed me, but not so much as my next discovery, when I came across a description of how fake pearls were first made from the shiny scales of fish similar to smelts. That fake pearls and smelts were so linked *in fact* and that I had felt such a link first *in story* was somehow thrilling. Such a "coincidence" is one of the signposts that leads me to the story.

Serendipity rarely takes the same path twice. It can't be routinized or manipulated. I did not begin the next story by playing an opera in the background and hoping for a direct link between the two. But serendipity plays in nearly every piece I write. Without it, I would lose a major motivation for writing.

When I am writing, I feel the presence of a poem, an essay, or a story. I expect the needed ideas to appear and associate in a way that unfolds the work at hand and transforms me, somewhat like Prigogine's molecules. Naturally, some will say this is a chicken-or-egg question. Somehow, they will say, all the rules and schemata of story are working together with the personal subconscious to bring about the story. There is no story "out there." The story is formulated, constructed, by the rational mind working just below the level of full awareness. Serendipity is simply the result of the hidden tangle of nerves and firing of neurons. Perhaps. This is one view. But it is not the paradigm that engages me in writing. How I think of the creative process—how it feels to me— impacts significantly on the work. It matters how I perceive the creative process. Creativity and science researchers often defend their paradigms by saying something along the lines of, "A chemical analysis of soup is not expected to taste like soup." Translation: An analysis of creative process shouldn't be expected to feel like the creative process. But what help is it to artists if science explains away the very inspiration behind their work? Certain ways of thinking about creativity feed the work; other ways dull the taste of the experience.

Artists must find and articulate for themselves the "feel" of their own creative endeavors. And critics and researchers must trust and respect the "feel" of doing art as the very essence of process.

Fundamental to knowing individual creative processes is an uncontrived intimacy with the artist's ground and with how she stands on that ground.

GROUNDING

When I read literature or essays that move me, I feel pulled to find out more about the author. Why? Because of the persistent belief that the source of the work is the writer and if I explore the source, I'll get a firmer grasp on the essence of the work. Wrong. The sad truth is that I can't ever remember not being at least a little disappointed. Most often, I feel a writer's work is her best self, where she yearns to be, but isn't quite yet. The work says something powerful to me, but indulging my curiosity in the author's personality will invariably weaken the very message I was seeking to strengthen. The work is bigger than the artist.

> Today my first published essay appeared. I have been worrying about the title all week. I kept picturing different versions in print. But when I saw the essay today, what first caught my eye was my name in bold black letters at the bottom. That familiar group of letters looked all wrong, intrusive. For some odd rea-

son I had not thought about seeing my name in print (not that I didn't consider it at other times!). Somehow I imagined the essay being read for itself, unattached to a person. I think I know now why people write anonymously or under assumed names. My father has always said, "You are your own person. I didn't make you." My life is full of his influence, yet he somehow knows I am something more than his child—with a name of my own. I feel that my essay should be marked by its title—and not my name. (Journal)

Years after this experience, I read of E. M. Forster's saying that literature "wants not to be signed." It hit home.

There's something pure about anonymity. If the writer forgets herself as she works, the reader, in turn, will forget the author while he reads. When the reader can engage directly with the work, he is able to forget himself as well. Personalities, ego, are out of the way, allowing the work a voice of its own. First the anonymous writer and then the anonymous reader open themselves to something other, something new.

Writing "wants not to be signed." The writer wants to get out of the way, to become a transparency for a new creation. Of course, the paradox is that when a writer or artist truly disappears into the work, she finds herself, takes on sharpened individuality. When a writer consistently and truly loses herself, her work does not need signing; every phrase, every metaphor, cries her name. Always the paradox.

Sometimes people identify their motive to create as self-expression—as though art's purpose were to validate a self, extend a self, or teach one about oneself. But a writer must give herself up to the characters and the story in the same way that an actor must lose herself in the part she plays. Creation requires that we throw ourselves away.

In my twenties, I wanted to be a writer. Actually, as James Michener put it (in Winokur, 10), I didn't want to be a writer so much as I wanted to *have been* a writer. I wanted to have a book in print. I thought of writing as a way to extend myself, a way to define myself. I did not know that the reason to write stories was to *escape* the hungry yet never satisfied ego.

But in my thirties, a more balanced view of writing and ego surfaced while I was talking to myself in my journal:

"Writers have at least a chance at understanding themselves."

"So what? Like there's something special to understand? Sounds a little self-absorbed to me."

"But there must be something to the old precept, 'Know thyself.'"

"Well, maybe, but it sure doesn't take being a writer to know yourself."

"Is one's self so easy to know? Is it just a matter of being conscious?"

"All I know is there isn't much good in being self-conscious. I can think of things a lot more productive than sitting around thinking about your 'self.' Talk about depressing."

"Hey! That's it! You don't know yourself by focusing on your 'self.' You know yourself—well, sort of from side glances—like when you spot yourself unexpectedly in the window glass sometimes? And you think, hey, who's that? And you see yourself as if for the first time? You *catch* yourself. I think that's how it works."

(Journal)

Writing, like all true art, is window glass. It absorbs our self-conscious self, but reflects our unknown inner self. It gives the excuse, the time, the space for quiet reflection and profound thought, for losing self. And in these still waters sudden reflections appear to show us ourselves—and others—mirrored in ways we don't recognize as "us." We catch ourselves unawares in sideways glances. "Knowing thyself" is not the point. It's a side reflection.

We need to know ourselves as writers, artists, parents, children, citizens. But we don't need to focus on knowing ourselves. (What a relief.) Instead we focus on serving the work—listening to the voice, obeying especially when its risky, entering in by giving ourselves up to the writing.

Willa Cather, in her preface to *The Country of the Pointed Firs and Other Stories* by Sarah Orne Jewett, portrays giving up self as the "gift of sympathy."

It is a common fallacy that a writer . . . can . . . [improve] upon his subject-matter, by using his "imagination" upon it and twisting it to suit his purpose. . . .

If he achieves anything noble, anything enduring, it must be by giving himself absolutely to his material. And this gift of sympathy is his great gift; is the fine thing in him that alone can make his work fine. He fades away into the land and people of his heart, he dies of love only to reborn again.

Such sympathy and empathy enjoin response more than creation.

Ear Training

One Tuesday afternoon during a blizzard, my piano teacher, Mrs. Potter, played a low C on the piano. As I listened, she hummed middle G. Then she stopped humming G and played the C again. I heard the G tone. It was not my imagination. It was in the air and always had been every time that low C was played. My ear had never known. Once I heard it, I couldn't un-hear it. G is an overtone of C. Every note sounds several overtones. Without the overtones, the note would sound flat. Each note gets its turn at being the primary sound, but each needs all the others to make it rich and full.   (Journal)

An overtone is a sympathetic response to another note. We could be scientific and refer to the alignment of the wavelengths of sound vibrations, but we would be saying essentially the same thing. Creativity requires that we perceive resonances.

Much of creating is simply response. It's accepting

what comes and responding to it. It's not a whining search for some lost ideal. You think when you renovate a house that at last you'll get what you've been dreaming of all these years. But you don't. The best that happens is you give creative response to whatever flies in your face. The finished product is a surprise, a discovery, an evolution. It is never *the plan*.

Like Willa Cather, we need appreciation and response. This sympathetic ground is the artist's attitude, the way she stands in relation to her work—as servant rather than creator. It may not be everyone's ground, but it is my ground. The objective observation of the empirical scientist will never survey this ground. His blunt tools cannot detect its substance. In a 1989 interview in the *Pacific Sun*, Huston Smith, an avid fan of science as well as a professor at the Graduate Theological Union in Berkeley, says,

> Because science turns on the controlled experiment and we can only control what is *less* than us, science can only show us things that are less than we are. If there are things greater than we are—more intelligent, better, God, angels—the scientific method ipso facto will never be able to point them out. (3)

Many researchers approach creativity as purposeful invention. I do my writing as discovery. If it is true that ideas "happen" to us, I feel better prepared to receive them as a servant and listener, as a discoverer rather than an inventor. When words, metaphors, visions, come as gifts in unpredictable ways, they seem necessary to a reasoned approach *after* they have been written or spoken.

An artist who follows her work by intuition stands on ground as sure and solid as the empirical scientist; but it is separate ground. Huston Smith says,

> [A]ll life requires faith . . . skeptics live by faith every day. Theirs is scientism, the dogmatic faith that the way science gets at truth is the only adequate, the only reliable way and that only what turns up on the viewfinder of science is real. . . . The problem is to develop within oneself an informed and responsible faith rather than a blind . . . faith. And the blunt truth is that there's no litmus test to indicate where that line between responsible and informed—you might say mature—faith stops and credulity and gullibility begin. (3)

Susan Griffin's personal account of the impact of intuition on her life and writing echoes my own feelings about writing and the growing awareness of a personal creative experience:

> Synchronisities, the voices of trees, rivers, the wind, coincidental openings of books, a larger knowledge that seemed available to me only through "intuition" . . . all these in my writing of the book changed me so

that in my acts, in my daily acts, I was no longer a child
of the age of science and rational thought.   (119)

A child of intuition. Many artists throughout the ages
have named childlike vision a requisite for their work.
Even to his last days, old Walt Whitman sustained a childlike fancy. (On the other hand, maybe it was his childlike
fancy that sustained old Walt.)

How strange that we spend our childhood years trying to gain adulthood and our adult years trying to recap-
ture lost childhood. But while most children succeed at
growing into adults, few adults grow into childlikeness.

Childlikeness is not childishness. Our culture works
hard at developing adultlike qualities and discarding
childish thought and behavior. That is right and good.
However, mature character should not cancel the progress of childlikeness, but support its continuing development. Sometimes, the very old are the ones who cherish
the essence of childlikeness:

Dicken

When I was sixteen, Dicken skipped with me all the
way down Fifth Avenue to 51st Street. I skipped because I was a visitor to the city and none of my friends
would ever know. I didn't wonder then why *he* skipped. I
was just happy to have such a youthful grandfather.

Twenty years later, after my grandmother died,
Dicken went with us to the Smithsonian Air and Space
Museum. Near the end of the day I sat with him on a

bench under one of the space shuttles. "It's wonder-ful," he sighed. (He said that often those days.) I asked him how he'd liked some of the different exhibits. His answer surprised me: "It's so comforting." We just held hands.

Months later I visited him in his apartment. When his daughters or granddaughters came, he usually asked one of us to sleep in the bed that had belonged to my grandmother. He would often wake at odd hours of the night because his schedule, now freed from work, allowed him to sleep whenever he wished. One night I was wakened by his soft voice. "Winnie-the-Pooh, Winnie-the-Pooh . . . They're changing guards at Buckingham Palace, Christopher Robin went down with Alice." He wasn't dreaming and I didn't interrupt his purposeful narration, but joined his reliving of the sounds and images of three generations of child-hood—his own, my mother's, and mine. During that night, he recited scraps of poems he had committed to memory as a young man.

Revisiting Winnie-the-Pooh with him reminded me of our long-forgotten skip down Fifth Avenue. I thought of the past-middle-aged man and the young girl who had a whole life before her. I realized that what that girl, and the woman she became, treasured about this man—this responsible man who had given up writing for law in order to support his family—what I treasured was his pure childlikeness. I felt honored, sure that his business partners and friends never knew what I knew. This childlikeness did not diminish his manhood or his lawyerly ways. It crowned them.

(Journal)

Now, I think I know why the Air and Space Museum comforted Dicken. As he sat surrounded by the history of aviation—from one man's passion for the freedom of flight to a nation's singular commitment to walk the moon—I think Dicken detected his link to something transcendent. He felt the awe and grandeur of accomplishments beyond man's capacity. At that moment, something reminiscent of his father's strong hand and his mother's loving arms touched him. His wonder was that of a child's, only extended, expanded, deepened by adult years.

This *adult* childlike wonder is full of gratitude, sacredness, potential, unfathomable meaning, innocence, faith, beauty, mystery. It is a humbled persuasion that after all is said and done, something big lurks behind the greatness of humanhood. While it is child*like*, it is not the same as the child's wonder, although it springs from that. The seed of adult childlikeness grows in the child, to ripen sometime in adulthood. The tragedy is that the concerns of adult life usually blight the full flowering of childlikeness.

I know I must not allow these childlike qualities to be smothered under adult cares, intellectual argument, or materialism. False intellect, like a fifth-grade bully, crushes them. True intellect respects them.

It's okay to chair the board meeting with businesslike organization, attention to detail, and a certain personal toughness and then go home to watch *Anne of Green Gables*, thoroughly enthralled by its sweetness and goodness. It's okay to read *The Runaway Bunny* in the morning (without a child on my lap) before grabbing a briefcase and heading to work.

This ground—this sympathetic, intuitive, self-losing, childlike, and faithful attitude—attracts other related qualities. Many of them are identified in a book about mystical fancy in children's literature by James Higgins:

> A work of mystical fancy for children has a combination of distinct qualities: it appeals to the heart; it is intuitively conceived, placing meditative demands upon the reader; it reflects the reality of a spiritual world; it reaches for a feeling of beyondness.... (103)
>
> Writers like MacDonald, Hudson, Saint Exupéry, Tolkein, Lewis and others are men stunned by the awesome beauty of the universe ... with strong appetites for the wonderful. They are sad men too, knowing as they do, how difficult it is to satisfy the appetites of the heart. The sadness that pervades their books is the joyful sadness of mortal men reaching for the immortal. (104)

The fairy tale, like the child, is a wildflower. It thrives

on a hillside of uncultivated innocence, nourished by
the elemental passions beneath the sod. These are the
passions which contribute to the sacredness of man,
without which man would cease to be. Not the least of
these passions is a feeling for a world which lies somewhere hidden underneath the physical world to which
the senses give evidence. (4)

The foundation of all these qualities lies in the passion for birth and rebirth—for wet, slippery newness. Am
I willing to rent my womb to this newness? Can I bear
that state of mind where the strange becomes familiar
and the familiar wonderful?

An appetite for the wonderful and beautiful, the joyful sadness, spirituality reaching for the immortal, faith,
innocence, childlikeness, wisdom more than knowledge,
an ever-affirming voice for the sacredness of life, prayer,
and revelation—this overflowing cascade of language is
enough to *cloy* most people's desire for inspiration.

I am embarrassed to admit that these words thrill me,
that I never can get enough of being moved by meaning
or transported by new insight into deeper sacredness and
purpose. I am consumed with "holy hunger." Sometimes
I think it's an eating disorder of the soul; sometimes I
think it's life itself.

PART TWO

— ❦ ❦ ❦ —

Out of the Jungle,
Into the Garden

❦ FIVE ❦

Possessing the Garden

When I first began to observe my creative processes, unforeseen complexities and confusions seized my reasoning abilities. It was nearly impossible to separate the parts, steps, routines, and methods that "process" implies. Within a few days, the work grew tedious and overwhelming. Disgruntlement at overcognitized academic theories, flowcharts, ordered steps to creation—all focusing on the surface of creative work—gnawed at me.

I am grateful now that my intent to research my creativity veered away from analyzing the minutiae of rational thought processes. Instead, intuition and natural inclination guided me to focus more generally on the felt experience of creation, which in turn led me to delve into deeper waters fed by other ways of knowing. By clinging to the elements of creativity, I was able to maintain a simplified approach to processes. But I know that creativity is actually a wild jungle of psychological, physiological, spiritual, philosophical, intellectual, unconscious, and conscious processes with mysterious unknowns and trackable knowns, the familiar and the strange. Now, only at the end of my journey, I see that when I entered the jungle, it was never intended that I explore the whole, wild thing but that I see what I needed to see, what was helpful to my work and life.

True, the tearing apart of creative processes by cognitive psychologists not only may be of little interest to artists but can actually harm their work if they adopt and attend to such conceptions of creation. But just as harmful may be the artist's overzealous desire to know her creative processes and elements past the point where such knowledge aids and supports her work. Peering into the jungle too long or too far—forcing knowledge before its time or need—ensnares the artist in webs of confusion and distraction. We should not raid the jungle but approach it as guests. It has much to yield that will help us in our work. And it has much to keep that may distract or harm our work.

POSSESSION RIGHTS

After explorers staked
their claims,
Trappers skinned
and traded its wealth,
Soldiers burned it
for the ambitions of war,
Woodsmen thinned it
for warmth of hardwood,

Farmers cleared it
for grazing pasture,
Industrialists heaped it
with waste and stench.

Then—when the forest was spent—
Only then
Came a poet.

Beside the dead forest
he laid a garden
to whisper blessings.

Fruit and flower flourished.
Finally disowned,
the forest drew its first breath.   (Anonymous)

Like the forest, my creative jungle is not land to be possessed.

While it calls for exploration at times, the jungle ultimately begs to be left alone. We cannot constantly observe how we work and continue to produce creatively. The watching tends to solidify a flowing, changing, infinite process. I feel impelled now to let go of what I learned and trust that what needs to stay with me will. The artist's responsibility is to encourage the jungle's invigoration—not by examining, poking, perpetually observing it and then trying to fix it, but by planting a small garden alongside.

And this is the unexpected garden we tend: its fruit is creative expression, its fertile soil is why we write, its weed is discouragement.

We encourage the complicated, interdependent eco-system of creativity by the very works of creative expression it engenders. However, the goal behind creativity research is useful methods, approaches, behaviors, attitudes that can be taught or somehow enhanced by human intervention or manipulation. But many artists believe intuitively that their best teacher is the work itself. As we attend to our work and look to the side to see what it is teaching, we will naturally gather what we need of the jungle behind the work.

Although I've found my research constructive and enlightening, I cannot maintain that it has made me a better or more creative writer or changed any harmful habits or processes. But along the way it has revealed what is important and potent in my life and writing. And it has opened to me the sacred hiddenness of the creative process that must be respected.

We must frequently affirm a place as writer or artist. Gaining a purposeful vision of our work includes an unfolding understanding of why we write and patient uprooting of discouragement. These will do more to invigorate the source of our creative work than any other labor.

❧ ❧ ❧

A WRITER'S GARDEN

The most important inhabitant of the garden is the creative work. It is the fruiting vine of the garden that requires trimming and training. It rambles. It would rather ramble in its profusion of green than produce fruit. That was one of my problems with writing. I just wrote. And wrote. The writing tumbled in a rangy mess with no design or purpose. I told myself I was pumping up my writing skills by trying diverse genres—poetry, essays, long and short stories, personal letters, letters to the editor, reviews, radio commentary, journals. But the realization that finely cut and polished pieces were rare made me squirm. I needed concentrated focus. At first, I thought it best to focus on a specific genre. Soon, I realized other possible focus points: message, purpose, subject, context.

However, we do not simply choose a focus and overlay it on our work. I am learning to heed intuitive guidance and accept the logic of events that lead me to my place as a writer. It has helped me to think of my career as I do a poem or story: to feel that intuition is leading me toward a place that is already established. If it is true of poems, might it not be true of a life as well? If such thinking serves creative expression, might it not also serve personal expression?

And now that I know the value of troubling and the intelligence behind good tension in my creative process, I see that these operate in my life, too. When a submission is rejected, when my abilities fall short of my desires, when too many deadlines deaden my zeal, I know that troubling is the mode of chaos that seeks a new cosmos, that a pattern and rhythm will develop that will carry my work forward.

Dispersed focus suggested I expand my sense of

place. I had unconsciously accepted that once I had published a book, I would do another, then another. I would be a career writer. But now my concept of writing is much broader. I see that I am writing whenever I carefully piece a sentence to console a friend. Or when I allow a thought to age and ripen before blurting it out. I am writing when the tree sparrow's song matches unexpected words within me. I see how I will always write, but I accept and look forward to unimagined surprises. And they include the possibility of my place as a true amateur—one, after all is said and done, who writes for the pure love of it.

The tension is perfect: while I know my place is established, I also understand that it is unfolding, developing, never static or fixed. I am comforted and exhilarated at once.

But to be successful, this philosophy requires a sure discipline that is still taking root within me. I have to listen to intuition consistently and then obey. Obedience sharpens and fortifies intuition. Intuition forged in daily acts of obedience and trust is not some airy, ephemeral cloud.

The desire and inspiration to obey the voice of intuition, whether it appears during meditation or interrupts busy activity, is strengthened by attention. I find if I don't attend to intuition, it fades from my life. So I try to affirm daily the validity of intuition, acknowledge my desire to obey it, and recognize the benefits such obedience brings.

The soil in the garden supports the fruit-bearing vine. Knowing why I write is the soil of my work. And keeping the soil sweet and free of pollutants is fundamental to a healthy writing life. While compiling thoughts for this book, I wrote often to discover why I write.

I first began to write to save as well as savor life. I collected piles of quotes from people who found the words to say what I believed in my wordless heart. Then I wrote down words from my own experience. Our house was full of little slips of scrap paper, some yellowed by age, some with drink spills. I think I was trying to collect and save my sense of what life should be.

I've swallowed something too fast. I try to cough it up again in order to chew it more. Life goes by so fast, and I miss the full meaning of its events. I want to chew on life, regurgitate it and really taste it. Cud—I'm into cud. I want to slow life down and look longer and more closely. But I don't really want to analyze it, tear it apart, do damage. I just want to hold it whole in my mouth and suck on it. Like a true baby with no teeth. Maybe that's a problem. I don't actually chew on life, I suck on it. I'm a baby, an immature mind. A mind that's satisfied to suck and gum its way through life, rather than masticate, pull it apart, shred it, get everything I can from it. But hey, maybe that's not a bad way to go through life.

I don't think I write to communicate to others. I write to tell myself something I don't know. The better you tell it, the better you understand it.

I write for the "first-time high." That peak experience of discovering something (maybe something everyone else already knows) for myself.

Writing's a way to figure things out—to find answers by coming around through the back door. Writing leads me, sometimes gently, sometimes by the ear, to discovery.

I write for the same reason I read: to find words that tell me what I think, what I really believe.

I write for transformation.

Writing touches my mind to the core of things. It feels like a great deep breath. Writing gives me the chance to sink deep into a comfy, cozy mind. It's more like that than hard analysis. (But writing helps me analyze, too).

My mind always feels unfinished. It's a great feeling to "finish" a piece of writing at least.

I write to say things I can't say out loud. Or things no one around me really wants to listen to.

I write to get to the bottom of unconscious thought that's bubbling up in life problems—relationships, health, societal debates, political issues, art issues—all these are fundamentally human issues—related to the workings of the psyche. We live in a mental construct. We share some overlapping borderlands and we share a deep center. I'm trying to explore those overlaps and center by looking into my own mental struggles. So I use my writing to come to grips with life.

But more and more I write to praise life, particularly nature and its power to renew and hearten human beings. And I praise humanity's tiny triumphs. The grains of sand that tell a world; the flower that holds heaven in its arrangement of petals.

I just want to be part of the conversation.

Something's trying to break into my world. I'm a midwife. It's my duty to welcome the new thing. No, I'm more a rented womb. I feel special. It comes to me because it chooses me.

I write for play. Wordplay. The play of metaphors and images. It's my backyard.

I write in order to see.

My hand itches; I scratch it. My mind itches; I write.

Writing for me is like cleaning windows. Through the clouded window I see shadows of things moving. I'm curious, I want to see them better. They're not just shadows. They have voices and are calling me. So I write and write and write until the view pleases me, or until the voices teach me something. It's a release. Perhaps it's like this for the painter and composer?

The truth is I write because I can't sing. If I had a choice, I'd be a singer-songwriter. But I like my family too much to subject them to such air pollution.

(Journal excerpts)

The developing vision of a writing life has as much to do with weeds as with soil and fruitful vines. Picking through the weeds of discouragement tells us plenty about why we write and leads us to how we might write. Reviewing my journals over a period of time, I realized my discouragement occupied two camps: disgust and impatience with my abilities compared with those of master writers and a feeling that a writing life lacked accomplishment. Attending to such thoughts led to more purposeful writing direction.

I read Annie Dillard and I'm so impressed—and so *de*pressed. How can I encourage myself to continue with the likes of her floating around all the bookstores and libraries?

First of all I have to lower the flag. I've got my standard waving wildly in the rarefied, upper stratosphere. No wonder I'm getting blown to bits. I'm not going to be Dillard or Nabokov or Barry Lopez or Madeleine L'Engle. I'm just going to be me—whatever that turns out to be. It's okay. Call me a slug, but the truth is, I don't feel the ambition to be a great writer. I just want an opportunity to write and make steady progress.

So, there. I'm entitled to write because I want to. I feel better.

So many authors spit one book out after another. Boy, why can't I do that? What am I lacking? Motivation? Chutzpah? Time in the labor camp? Dues?

I'm having trouble calling myself a writer. And not just because of the prolific Shakespeares. Whenever people ask me what I do, and after some pause I say "I write," they usually blurt back, "Oh yeah, me too. Just finished the third chapter of a novel I've been working on." Or, "Boy, my computer is just full of stuff I'd love to publish. I've got the time to write, but—hey—there's not time to find publishers!"

Nothing difficult. Nothing special. Everyone writes. It's like breathing. Next time they ask, I'll say I'm a breather.

As beginners we have this trumped up, inflated sense that we *can* write. We read others' work and think, "I can do that." So we begin to write. We think what we've done is pretty good. But then, readers—teachers, friends, brothers and sisters (in my case, my grandfather)—don't quite see it that way. Later, we come across the writing and think "Gee, I thought *this* was good?" We're relieved we didn't show it all over town. Pretty soon, everyone's looking good except us. We see talent everywhere, but not in ourselves. At this crucial point, we either give up or try too hard. We circulate; we imitate; we stay up all night; we haunt all the right places; we act like writers and wallow in a writer's world hoping it will rub off; we take on new personae to attract some good ideas. But good ideas, like people, see right through us and they are repulsed by all this silly behavior. When we give up the costumes and airs, we finally come to ourselves. Then we have something to say in our own way.

(Journal excerpts)

Many a discouraging word littered the pages of my journals. But when I paid them some attention, they taught me. I could see through imposed, false ambitions as not belonging to me. My arms opened wide to accept all levels of writing from all degrees of commitment as valid in their own way. I learned to accept my limitations with a little grace and hope, to laugh at myself and like myself better for it. I began to appreciate the singular road that lies before me as good and satisfying.

These journal thoughts also put the occupation of writer in its place: nowhere in particular. We each redefine what "writer" means; it does not define us.

❦ ❦ ❦

EXPLORING CREATIVE JUNGLES

The garden we tend is infinite and eternal. We may lack the desire or the time to hunt in the jungle—to thrash or pick our way through the complex, knotty, and enigmatic processes behind our creativity. And such a search is not necessary for everyone. I needed it in order to continue writing.

Does intense observation sap creativity? At least for me, talking about it, thinking about it for extended periods, weakened the sense of its power. The words "inspiration" and "intuition" and "sacred," so sweet in thought, have lost their taste in the mouth and on paper. They need to rest in the wordless experience of creating in order to regain their power.

Too much observing and rationalizing drains the deep of its mystery and mysticism. And this is the danger of observing ourselves too closely. When we observe to understand, to explain, isn't the end to make what we observe mundane? But when we observe to create, to express, isn't the end to magnify mystery, wonder, awe? Perhaps here lies the very problem: by observing to understand and put forth my creative process, I assumed the role of scientist and renounced my place as artist.

Predictably, looking at my creative processes soon became habitual. I found myself more interested in—even obsessed with—thoughts about inspiration and intuition and less interested in doing the creative work that springs from inspiration and intuition. This was unnatural. I was out of joint with identity. I found an effective balance in "noticing"—simply catching certain aspects of creation out of the corner of my eye. That seems to me the only possible and valid way for an artist to research the processes behind her creative efforts.

If I had been able to focus directly on the jungle, I would have been blind to the real work of writing the story. There would have been nothing to watch!

If we do not hear a call to investigate our creative jungle, then we do not need to. However, it is necessary for us all to tend the garden. When an artist finds and evolves a personal vision of her work, it sustains her creative energy rather than saps it. Without this purposefulness, the work must shrivel. The two go hand in hand. We should continually rediscover why we write. We should attend to doubts and discouragements in order to transform them into the building blocks of our purpose, rather than let them rot our inspiration and energy while we accept them or work around them. We need to spend what may sometimes seem an inordinate amount of time simply caring for our vision. This caretaking is the soul of our work.

When Moses approached God saying, "Show me your glory," he was told that no one could see God's face and live (Exodus 33:18). Myths have long warned against looking reality directly in the eye.

Without light we cannot see, yet light blinds. The paradox exists only in the limitation of the words, though. The resolution lies in *how* we see. We see *by* light, not *into* light. The mountain colors steal our breath when the sun is at our backs. But this same magnificence fades to dull gray when we look into the sun.

Writing is itself a light source. We do not look directly into it but by it.

The work of the writer is to see by the light of writing, not to look into or analyze the light source.

❦ SIX ❦

Suckers and Volunteers

When I finally weeded the flower garden sometime in August, I came upon a dreamy blue campanula luxuriating in the middle of the hostas under the maple trees. I had not planted it. The wind had carried the seed twenty yards from its parent on the south wall.

Gardeners call such accidental plants "volunteers." Good gardeners love the volunteers—leaving them to flourish or gently moving them to a better part of the garden. Evil gardeners pluck them up and cast them onto the compost pile.

Writing this book was like gardening. Volunteers kept springing up and surprising me. But the ground was crowded. So, for their own good I plucked them up and transplanted them here.

Sometimes plants put out so many shoots that the little branches sap all the food, leaving little for the fruit. If that's the case, the gardener has to prune. The "suckers" have to go for the sake of the fruit and the overall health of the plant.

Likewise, a piece of writing produces many side shoots that unless they are removed will sap the power of the writing. It's not that these shoots don't belong; it's just that there are too many for the writing to bear. I had to cut much from this book, but I saved some of the suckers.

🐞 🐞 🐞

A FEW NIPPED SIDE SHOOTS

Names

Don't call yourself a writer, especially to yourself. Find your other names: mother, brother, caretaker, child, seer, firestarter, joygiver, nurse, a worker for clarity, watcher, waker, gardener, praiser, thinker, player. Then add "writer" as a surname. First names tell who you are. Your surname tells what tribe you belong to. Think of your first names often and find new ones. They give you breathing space, keep you large—like a trip to Wyoming.

Refraining from calling yourself a writer also damps the temptation to use your world and the people in it for your writing.

Severing the Vision

During a walk I was struck by a flock of blackbirds taking flight. Their upward drift reminded me of falling leaves in reverse. I decided to use the two images in a school project due the next day. I glued torn paper bits to a strip of fan-folded panels depicting blackbirds swirling upward and then metamorphosing into colorful falling leaves that landed gently in a pile. Delores, our teacher, asked me if I was pleased. I said no, the piece fell so far short of what I had felt. It couldn't communicate the vision's sweeping movement. Then she asked, "Could you not look at the work simply as the work and appreciate it for what it is?" This didn't help at the time, but it stuck with me. I couldn't separate the work from the high feeling of the vision. But recently, I located the fan-folded art and, even with its faded colors and worn edges, it seemed surprisingly fresh. Now I appreciated it in two dimensions: first, as a happy, primitive piece of art; and second, as a sudden, powerful reminder of that day's flight of spirit. Time had severed the art from the vision. Then the black and colorful images were allowed to speak to me.

Truth

Don't try to be consistent. Just tell the truth.

We sit amid the truth; we do not comprehend it. It holds us; we do not hold it, intellectually or otherwise. If we see truth as finite, then we can contain it. If we perceive it as infinite, it must contain us.

Because truth is constantly unfolding from its own infinity, we will always feel its mystery. And mystery requires faith. If we believe material science cancels mystery and therefore obviates faith, our tiny, finite science is doomed.

Mindfulness, Wisdom, and Intuition

Intuition is *not* a soft way of knowing. It requires rigor, discipline, alertness, and courage. I have said that intuition is sharpened through obedience. I mean that through a willingness to stand on our intuition we allow ourselves the mistakes or proof that will guide us to discern true intuition. Intuition is not what people often describe as wishful thinking, subconscious will, fearful presentiments. These, in fact, mask and divert intuition.

Neither is intuition all acceptance, "whatever will be will be." Intuition is intelligent discernment. It aids us in rejecting erroneous thoughts, as well as in accepting right ideas.

So the mind guided by intuition does not shun reason but lifts and supports it. It is not a vague mind, though it often follows thought that is vague to reason. Because of reason's blindness, intuition must be honed and strengthened to do the job reason cannot—to see beyond the seeing.

Dear Mom . . . Love, Geoffrey

Geoffrey Godsell, a well-known international reporter, fell on a foolproof way to handle muddled writing. One day, when he couldn't figure out where the writing was going, he yanked the paper out of the typewriter, rolled in a fresh piece, and began, "Dear Mom." As he headed down to "Love, Geoffrey," he wrote, in simple, plain language what he had been trying to say all along. Sometimes when I'm snagged in the writing, I just change my audience—anyone but me.

The Writer's Room, the Writer's Cell

I think of the whole world as my writing room. Most of my ideas and inspiration come outside the office. I have to have paper handy to jot mnemonic phrases down until I can get to the office to write. I like going to the office when I feel inspired. But I *hate* going when I'm struggling with a piece (a good part of the time) or when nothing in particular inspires me. Then, the whole world seems a garden and my office is a cell. A place for torture and deprivation. Why would I possibly commit myself there?

All right. So I painted the walls a different color, hung new pictures, added plants. Got rid of my desk chair; brought in a wicker rocker. Opened the windows even though a light snow drifted onto the papers. I invited the world in: "Ple-e-e-ase. Save me!"

But in the end, *this* is what works: I use the mail (often the high point of a writer's day) to get myself to the chair. Today it's a bunch of spring mail-order catalogs. I'll just get through these and then I'll leave. The catalogs grow stale, and without thinking I flip on the computer. I'll just erase a few garbage files. Then I do a word count on an essay. Not so bad. I'm feeling better. I'll just format next week's reviews. I won't read the books yet, just get down all the standard stuff—author, title,

ISBN number. One small thoughtless job leads to another. My room seems friendlier. Its walls begin to widen. Soon I'll be able to revise some old writing. Then I may even open a new file.

How to Know What Your Writing Means to You

Look first at when you write; if this doesn't satisfy you, then look at where you write; then what. Look into how you write only after trying the other three first. This painless procedure gradually leads you into deeper levels of your writing and will not tell you more than you need to know.

Talking Out Loud: When and When Not

I find talking out loud particularly effective while grocery shopping, driving in heavy traffic, doing my taxes—and while writing. Talking to myself aids concentrated focus by holding dispersed focus in balance. I usually say the same thing over and over again: "Now, *what* am I really trying to say here?" or "What is this conversation *really* about?" or "Where are all these words leading?"

However, there are times when writers must never talk out loud. Whenever I'm out with friends, I have to remind myself to clench my teeth when asked about my writing. Talk deflates the work, siphons off energy needed for writing. Whenever I have indulged other people's curiosity or my own desire to talk my writing through, I've been sorry. As yet unformed, my big thoughts always come out sounding obvious or less than coherent. As I babble on, I find myself wondering, why am I writing about this?

Talking my writing through with myself benefits and encourages the writing. But I can't carry on this conversation in a vacuum. Maintaining wide interests through reading and the media introduces into this conversation a varied assortment of points of view and suggests applications to challenge as well as beef up writing ideas. *Listening* more than talking to friends brings depth to this conversation with myself. (That's a hard one.)

How Writing Feeds Life

When I am working on deadline, writing drains me. I feel depressed because all I'm doing is writing. Everything's on hold until I meet the deadline. Then writing does not feed my life; it sucks it dry. But when I write in rhythm with all the other aspects of life—with family demands, walks and exercise, church and community, friends—the writing feeds me.

Hermit-ically Sealed? What Writing Does for Conversations with Real People

When I started writing full time, I noticed when I met people that my small-talk skills were waning. Every time I talked with anybody except a close friend, I felt like a hermit groping for the old ways of conversation. In the company of real people, I began to think this writing thing was perhaps not the best idea. I was beginning to feel more at ease in dialogue with fictional people.

After a few months, though, I was convinced that all heavyweight conversationalists should write. As a writer, I was becoming accustomed to revising, rethinking. Although I trust first thoughts or emotions, I don't trust first articulations of them. The more I write, the more I value aged, distilled ideas. Holding my tongue is no longer a major-muscle-group exercise. I listen better. Writing lets me say "I don't know" much more often in conversation.

Writing essays in particular heightens awareness of my own thought. My life and conversation draw specifically on what I've learned while writing. I am watching the writing forge life views. Other people do it other ways—through discussion, through simple reflection. This self-awareness sharpens my reading of other people.

Conversation II

Writing gives my thinking room, some air to breathe. It leads thoughts to their essences. More and more, it is the essence I want to speak. I want to dig through the soft layers of conversation to the hard, gold nuggets. I don't want to subject my partner to every detail of the process. I want shortcuts.

But no! A conversation is a joint discovery. It would not be fair to hide parts of the process from my partner. *If* conversation is a joint endeavor, then it's right to share the steps of the process. However, conversation is often *not* a sharing. Often, I am trying to figure something out, or she is. We don't need a conversation so much as a sounding board. That's when a partner should be silent. So the trick is to know the identity of an unfolding conversation. Is my partner discovering her own direction and inner thoughts?—then I need to give her the air. Or is it a joint exploration by the interaction of two minds in a productive tension?—then we need to share all the thoughts along the way.

Still, writing activates a desire to share gold rather than dross. And that is good.

The Cost of Words

Are words losing power? People throw 'em around as if they're free, as if they cost nothing. But the power behind words is integrity—not honesty, but soundness, unity (as in "integral," "integrated"). Words have to be tied to something substantial to carry weight. I pray my words are anchored in thoughts and deeds, but the truth is that words win more than their fair share of attention. And the cost of unanchored words is bone loss—the shrinking away of our very substance.

Finishing School for Writers

We are finishing even as we begin. As we lay down a phrase on paper, we are completing it—revising the words, adjusting the tone, sharpening the meaning, homing in on the frequency of the voice that grows perpetually clearer and nearer. Words and phrases ferry back and forth between our immediate perception and the complete thought or story. The gulf between potential and form shrinks.

Dancer Edward Villella said leaping and landing are one motion. "You must pass through down on your way up." Up needs down. Down needs up. Beginning and finishing are one motion. Beginning needs finishing as much as finishing needs a beginning.

So it's all right when we feel the need to perfect a word or phrase before proceeding. It's all right if in finishing an essay or a story scene, we find the premise of the work changing.

For a while I thought finishing was the stamp of wholeness, completeness. The written words are "finished" for various reasons: they're as good as they can be, the deadline is *now*, I'm just too sick of the work to continue. But the thoughts behind the writing are always on the way to becoming something new. The road, the words, end, but the thoughts move on without a hitch. The mind is ever unfinished. Perhaps finishing is not the point at all. Perhaps finishing has little to do with wholeness.

It helps me to know that each moment is whole. Completeness comes not by stringing together incomplete moments. Only wholeness begets wholeness. Tension stirs in the fact that each moment is both whole and part of a greater wholeness.

Light is both particles and waves; writing and life are discrete bits and continuous flow. We can have both. We can have finishing within our written pieces. We can have the wholeness of continuous flow in our writing experience.

THE BOOK IS FINISHED

And we can have endings. We long for them. Nothing satisfies like an ending—the end of the story, the end of the day, even the end of vacation. And no ending is so gratifying as the end of work. Such bliss, free of guilt and deserving of rest, visits most of us too rarely.

Writing is like running and dieting. The last ten pounds, the last half mile, the last revisions, seem to demand three times the determination. Ah, but the sweeter the finish line!

But unlike the dieter and the runner, the writer cannot see the finish line. She feels an urgency. All the elements of the book gather speed toward the whirlpool that will suck them into the end. But she cannot estimate when that will be. Suddenly, she's there, without a breath of word left.

She passes the book, like a baton, to the reader. She knows the reader will mine meaning and catch side thoughts that never occurred to her as the writer. So she gives up the book gratefully, trusting that its finishing is in good hands.

❦ BIBLIOGRAPHY ❦

Allen, Walter. *Writers on Writing.* Boston: The Writer, 1988.

Berends, Polly Berrien. *Whole Child/Whole Parent.* New York: Harper & Row, 1983.

Berry, Wendell. *Standing by Words.* San Francisco: North Point Press, 1983.

Beveridge, W.I.B. *The Art of Scientific Investigation.* London: Heinemann, 1957.

Bradbury, Ray. *Zen in the Art of Writing: Essays on Creativity.* Santa Barbara: Capra Press, 1989.

Briggs, John, and F. David Peat. *Turbulent Mirror.* New York: Harper & Row, 1989.

Calkins, Lucy McCormick. *The Art of Teaching Writing.* Portsmouth, N.H.: Heinemann, 1986.

Capra, Fritjof. *The Tao of Physics.* Berkeley: Shambala, 1975.

Csikszentmihalyi, Mihaly. *Flow: The Psychology of Optimal Experience.* New York: Harper & Row, 1990.

cummings, e. e. "i am so glad and very." In *Poems, 1923–1954,* 385–86. New York: Harcourt, Brace & World, 1968.

Dillard, Annie. *The Writing Life.* New York: Harper & Row, 1989.

Dossey, Larry, M.D. *Space, Time & Medicine.* Boston: Shambhala, 1982.

Elbow, Peter. *Writing with Power.* Oxford, U.K.: Oxford University Press, 1981.

―――. *Writing Without Teachers.* Oxford, U.K.: Oxford University Press, 1973.

Els, Susan McBride. "The Flying Horses." Novel in progress. Typescript.

―――. Journals, 1988–1992.

―――. Process notes, 1988–1992.

―――. "The Reader as Creative Partner." Typescript, 1989.

Finlayson, Donald Lord. *Michelangelo the Man.* New York: Tudor, 1936.

Fleishman, Paul. Press conference at the Boston Globe–Horn Book Awards ceremony. Springfield, Massachusetts, 1990.

Gallo, Delores. Graduate studies lecture at the University of Massachusetts at Boston, 1988.

Gardner, John. *The Art of Fiction.* New York: Random House, 1985.

Gleick, James. *Chaos: Making a New Science.* New York: Penguin, 1987.

Goldberg, Natalie. *Writing Down the Bones.* Boston: Shambhala, 1986.

Goswami, Amit. *The Cosmic Dancers: Exploring the Physics of Science Fiction.* New York: Harper & Row, 1983.

Griffin, Susan. "Thoughts on Writing: A Diary." In *The Writer on Her Work,* vol. 1, edited by Janet Sternburg, 107–20. New York: Norton, 1980.

Henri, Robert. *The Art Spirit.* New York: Harper & Row, 1984.

Higgins, James E. *Beyond Words: Mystical Fancy in Children's Literature.* New York: Teachers College, 1970.

Jewett, Sarah Orne. *The Country of the Pointed Firs and Other Stories.* Garden City, N.Y.: Doubleday, 1956.

Jung, C. G. *Modern Man in Search of a Soul.* New York: Harcourt, Brace & World, 1933.

Le Shan, Lawrence. *The Medium, the Mystic and the Physicist.* New York: Viking, 1974.

L'Engle, Madeleine. *A Circle of Quiet.* New York: Farrar, Strauss & Giroux, 1972.

Maher, John M., and Dennie Briggs. *An Open Life: Joseph Campbell in Conversation with Michael Toms.* Burdett, N.Y.: Larson, 1988.

McPhee, John. Radio interview with Terry Gross on WHYY Philadelphia's *Fresh Air*, 11 December 1989.

Moyers, Bill. Transcript (#BMSP-14) of PBS Television Program "Spirit and Nature." Aired on June 5, 1991.

Murray, Donald M. *Shoptalk: Learning to Write with Writers.* Portsmouth, N.H.: Heinemann, 1990.

Paterson, Katherine. *The Spying Heart.* New York: E.P. Dutton, 1989.

Plimpton, George, ed. *Women Writers at Work: The Paris Review Interviews.* New York: Penguin, 1989.

Polanyi, Michael. *Personal Knowledge: Towards a Post-Critical Philosophy.* Chicago: University of Chicago Press, 1958.

Prigogine, Ilya, and Isabelle Stengers. *Order out of Chaos: Man's New Dialogue with Nature.* New York: Bantam, 1984.

Rampal, Jean-Pierre. *Suite for Flute and Jazz Piano* record jacket interview. Columbia Records, M 33233, 1975.

Ratiner, Steven. Series of interviews with poets. *The Christian Science Monitor,* Aug. 21, Nov. 6, 1991; March 18, May 13, Dec. 9, 1992; March 3, May 26, 1993.

Rico, Gabriele Lusser. *Writing the Natural Way.* Los Angeles: J. P. Tarcher, 1983.

Sarton, May. *Writings on Writing.* Orono, Maine: Puckerbrush Press, 1980.

Shallcross, Doris J., and Dorothy A. Sisk. *Intuition: An Inner Way of Knowing.* Buffalo: Bearly Limited, 1989.

Shaw, Cynthia L. "A Writer's Debt to Her Father." *The Christian Science Monitor,* June 18, 1987, 31–32.

Smith, Huston. "A Healthy Disbelief." *Pacific Sun,* January 20, 1989, 2, 3, 8.

Spinelli, Jerry. Press conference for the Boston Globe-Horn Book Awards ceremony. Springfield, Massachusetts, 1990.

Sternberg, Janet, ed. *The Writer and Her Work.* 2 vols. New York: W. W. Norton, 1980, 1991.

Strickland, Bill. *On Being a Writer.* Cincinnati: Writer's Digest, 1989.

Sweeney, Louise. "Athol Fugard on the Power of Words." *The Christian Science Monitor,* December 7, 1989, 10–11.

Tolstoy, Leo N. *What Is Art?* Indianapolis: Bobbs-Merrill, 1960.

Ueland, Brenda. *If You Want to Write.* Saint Paul, Minn. Graywolf Press, 1987.

Vaughan, Frances E. *Awakening Intuition.* New York: Doubleday, 1979.

Winokur, Jon, ed. *Writers on Writing.* Philadelphia: Running Press, 1987.

Young, Ed. Press conference for the Boston Globe-Horn Book Awards ceremony. Springfield, Massachusetts, 1990.

Zinsser, William, ed. *Worlds of Childhood* and *Spiritual Quests.* Writer's Craft Series. Boston: Houghton Mifflin, 1988, 1990.